CareerMap

Discover your unique purpose

CareerMap

Discover your unique purpose

Cathy McCafferty-Smith

Edited by Emily Gehman; design by Kevin Mungons.

KNOW-U helps people of all ages and experiences discover their unique purpose, skills, talents, and strengths to find meaningful work and ministry opportunities. Founded in 2010 by Cathy McCafferty-Smith, Know-U began by helping people discover their unique purpose during a challenging economic recession.

know-u.info

Contents

1
Start Packing
Checkpoint #1: Know Your Skills
2
Know Your Personality
Checkpoint #2: Know Yourself
3
Why Skills & Accomplishments Matter
Checkpoint #3: Ten Accomplishments
4
Values: Your Energy Motivators
Checkpoint 4: Your Most Important Values
5
Your Unique Blueprint
Checkpoint #5: Embrace Your Quirks!
6
The Kaleidoscope of You
Checkpoint #6: Your Battery Chargers
7
Busting Internal Barriers
Checkpoint #7: Identify Your Internal Barriers
8
You—on Purpose
Checkpoint #8: Your Purpose Statement
9
Your Personal Board of Directors
Checkpoint #9: Your Personal Board of Directors
10
Net-Giving: Better than Networking
Checkpoint #10: Your Net-Giving

Introduction: Your CareerMap

IF YOU are like me, you may have picked up this book in curiosity and questioned, "I wonder if this would be a book that would be interesting, fun, helpful, and could it in some way *change my life?*"

My question to you is do you know that God has as a special assignment for only you, that will lead you to your unique purpose and calling which can lead to an energizing, meaningful life?

What do you want to be when you grow up? You've answered this question hundreds of times, likely, and probably differently almost every time. Among your answers may have been princess, football player, veterinarian, astronaut, doctor, or president. Maybe you've uttered all the above to unsuspecting aunts and uncles and other relatives.

But what do you say when someone asks you about your calling? Or what if they ask, "What is your purpose?" Are you at a loss for words? Do you go deer-in-headlights on them? Maybe you picked up this book in curiosity, wondering if it could be helpful or maybe even in some way change your life. But that's actually not the right question. The better question is: "What's so important to you that you need to do something about?"

This book and its exercises will help you answer this pivotal, life-changing question.

Friend, the fact that you hold this book in your hands as you ask these questions of yourself is not a coincidence. In fact, I don't really believe that coincidences are just random things that happen. I do, however, believe in divine appointments. Check out one of my favorite authors, SQuire Rushnell, and his God Winks series. His books illustrate the mini-miracles and clues that have happened to real people who did not immediately recognize the miraculous message confirming God's purpose in their lives.

When you lace together those small divine-appointment moments, you'll begin developing a roadmap for life. Most key to this process is Scripture and wise counsel of others, and these unexplainable mini-miracles are like little candles lighting the way to the next checkpoint.

"For we are God's handiwork, created in Christ Jesus to do good works, which God prepared in advance for us to do."

—*Ephesians 2:10*

Think You're Too Old for This?

You're not! Age has no bearing on what God has for our lives. In the Bible, Abraham, 100, and Sarah, 90, had a son that started a nation. And King Josiah was crowned at age 8. Clearly, God doesn't care what number your next birthday will bring. You're not too old and it's not too late.

If you're still alive, whether you're still working, semi-retired, retired, or volunteering, God still has a plan for you. Others still need your gifts and talents. This book is for you, too. You can reinvent yourself as many times as God asks. Your next journey is ahead, and this book will help you map it. Find a new way to continue what you love and serve others. If you are still breathing, God still has work for you to do!

God never gives up on ushering you to your levels of purpose as you learn and grow.

"For we are God's handiwork, created in Christ Jesus to do good works, which God prepared in advance for us to do" (Ephesians 2:10).

1 Start Packing

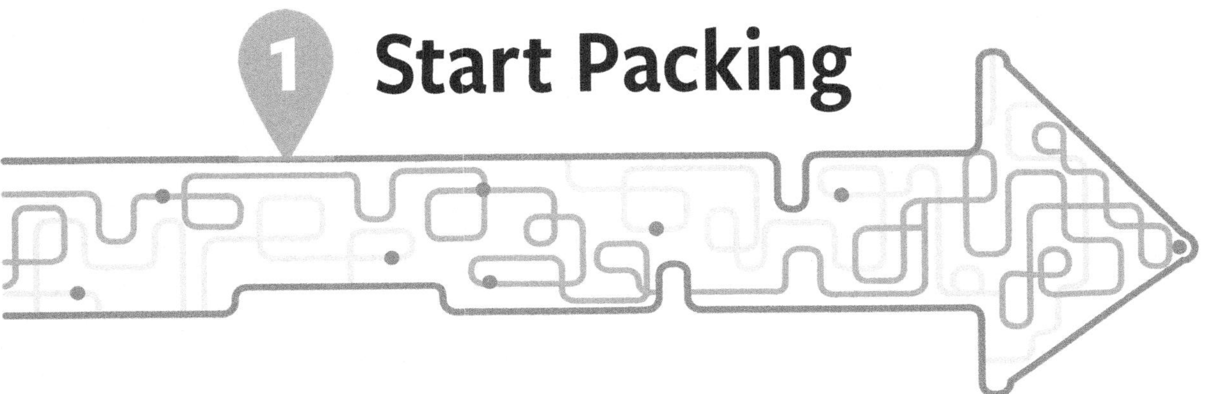

WHEN I WAS 5 years old, Mrs. Kelly, my kindergarten teacher, told my mother that she would feel comfortable leaving me (little Cathy) in charge of the class if she had to leave the room! Of course, my mom thought this meant I was bossy—but God meant it as a call to teach and lead. I still love to teach and lead groups!

What Mrs. Kelly said to me is still in my heart and is true for me. When others validate a skill, don't dismiss it.

When I was 12, shortly after I accepted Jesus and became one of God's kids, God gave me a verse that scared the bejeebers out of me!

"I will speak of your statutes before kings and will not be put to shame" (Psalm 119:46). Looking back, most of my time in the workplace and in churches has been shoulder-to-shoulder with senior leaders—kings, if you will.

I still remember when I was 15, sitting in my bedroom, when a quiet, inner voice said to me, "There ought to be someone who can help people figure out what God wants them to do with their lives."

And almost twenty years later, I realized that voice didn't say I needed someone; it said there ought to be someone. I realized that someone was me.

> "I will speak of your statutes before kings and will not be ashamed."
> —*Psalm 119:46*

In the decades since that realization, I've helped thousands of people from all walks of life and levels as a career coach, consultant, trainer, and human resources leader. And in those decades, I've seen many changes in the careers available and even the elimination of careers because of technological development. This change continues rapidly.

To keep up, emerging leaders are more willing to change jobs and "try them on" for short-term learning experiences and growth.

Gallup.com reports that 21% of millennials have changed jobs within the past year, and 60% of millennials say they are open to a different job opportunity. That's fifteen points higher than the percentage of non-millennial workers who say the same. Millennials are also the most willing to act on better opportunities: 36% report that they will look for a job with a different organization in the next twelve months, if the job market improves.

Personally, based on many interactions with young leaders and emerging leaders, I believe these experimentation trends are a result of seeking one's unique purpose.

So it makes sense to also revise our career and ministry-seeking methods to find new ways to manage this kind of rapid career turnover. We must accept the reality of frequent changes and learn how it will affect us both physically and emotionally. But it also pushes us to explore more deeply the spiritual aspects of who we are and not just what we do. Let's talk about that for a minute.

Who You Are

It's so easy to mix identity with profession, but that is dangerous. Who you are isn't tied to what you do. If it is, what happens when you don't do what you do anymore? What happens if you are laid off or let go, or you have an injury and can't work? What about retirement? None of those situations should affect or change the person you are—your character, your passions, and your purpose. But when you too tightly link your job with your identity, you set yourself up for a real identity crisis when faced with a career change.

Who you are cannot be defined by what you do. No, who you are is defined by something—Someone—much greater. Who you are aligns with your divine purpose in partnership with God.

◁ **Don't confuse who you are with what you do... set your sights on your greater purpose, for which God made you.** ▷

For Christians, our divine purpose is to glorify our Savior, Jesus Christ, with our talents and skills and to serve each other in whatever job, vocation, or career(s) we choose.

Don't confuse who you are with what you do. Keep your right perspective; set your sights on your greater purpose for which God made you, not just what you do for a paycheck.

Packing Your Skills Suitcase

Back to that rapid change in the workforce these days. How will you navigate our fast-paced and ever-changing world? Well, you need a toolbox. A Skills Suitcase, as I like to call it. It must be easily packed and ready to travel. Your skills must be identified for easy adaptations as you navigate career and ministry changes and move through various employment and service settings.

This book is a Skills Suitcase packing guide. Kind of like those travel magazines that tell you all about the best destinations and what to pack when you go there, this book will walk you through packing your Skills Suitcase. It's a how-to guide for 21st century career and ministry. Throughout these pages you'll discover who you are, what you're best at, what energizes you, and where you might be called to serve. It provides an inner search and external test-drive process to help you find all these things. It will include self-discovery and thought-provoking exercises to equip you for the road ahead—wherever it may take you!

God specially equipped you for the career changes you may encounter in life. He will increase your skills and talents and service as you mature. This process is for anyone at any age and for those making a change either by choice or by necessity. And the process applies to all career choices, including the stay-at-home career, full-time ministry, your career ministry in the workplace, or for service in retirement.

Christians are called to serve wherever we are and however old we may be (or not be)!

Know Your Skills

In order to pack your Skills Suitcase, you need to know your skills. That's a no-brainer.

Okay, so, what are your skills and talents?

Hmm? What's that you say? You don't know exactly? You're not sure what you would say if someone asked you that? It looks like we've got some work ahead.

Throughout these pages, we'll walk through a series of checkpoints on your CareerMap to discover your skills and what you are naturally suited for. I like to call this Know-U, the first *university* you should ever attend! It's the process of identifying your personality style, talents, skills, abilities, interests, values, and even your internal obstacles as you pack your suitcase and find your purpose.

Use this book to take notes as you discover new things about yourself and uncover your skills.

ProTip: Interview Strategy

"Tell me about yourself" is a common interview question. It sounds like an easy one until you get in the hot seat. Practice your answer—and rather than bragging about yourself, phrase it this way: "Instead of telling you about myself, may I tell you what others have said I do well?"

◁ Checkpoint #1: Know Your Skills ▷

Has anyone ever told you that you really have a knack for something? Or said they wished they could do it as well as you do?

And have you responded with something like, "Oh, that's no big deal!" Or are too embarrassed to say anything?

It *is* a big deal! You see, if others notice the good things you do and take the time to tell you, and you feel like you're barely even trying, that means it comes very easy to you. And if it's easy, it's a skill!

Let me give you some examples of things that others have said about me:

- You try to see both sides of an issue while caring for the people involved.
- You are good at telling stories and teaching through stories.
- You are great at sewing quilts and anything that has a variety of colors.
- You are an amazing public speaker and group facilitator.
- You are witty and quick on your feet, and you have a great sense of humor.
- You are a master networker.

These are from my personal, ministry, *and* professional parts of my life. Your list can be from any part of your life, too—not just your career. Let's start by creating a list of positive things others have said about you.

What five things do others say you're good at?

1. ....
2. ....
3. ....
4. ....
5. ....

For each exercise, you'll have the opportunity to reflect on the experience. Reflection is important; thinking deeply about what really matters to you is key. We'll be doing this in small chunks along the way and put it all together later to create your CareerMap!

Jot down your thoughts and feelings about those five things you listed above. As you think about what others have said about you, how does that make you feel? Which words or phrases touch your heart?

What do you think about what they have said? Do you agree? Why or why not?

2 Know Your Personality

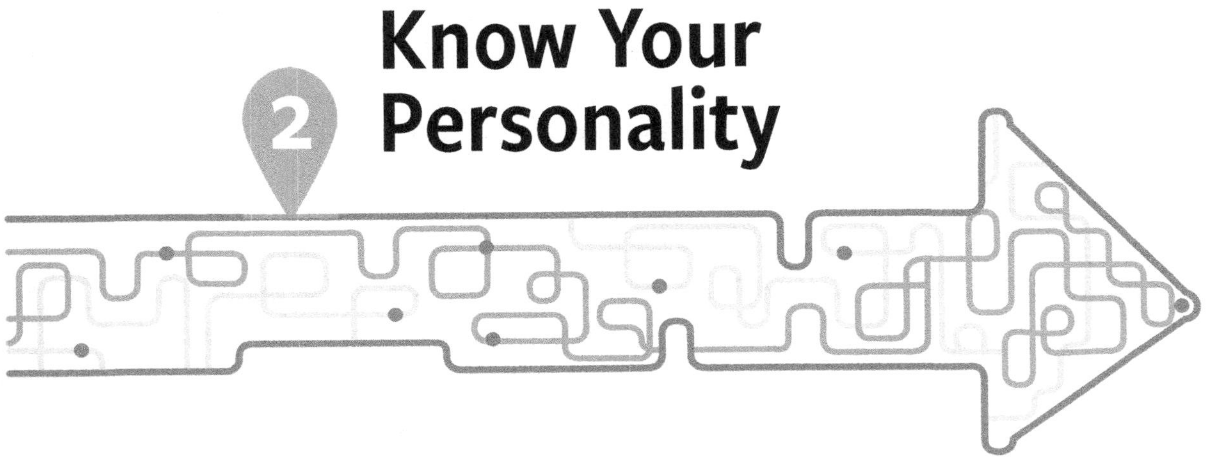

MRS. KELLY saw potential leadership skills in me. She identified a part of my personality—something that develops in all of us long before we know what it is.

The more I learned about different personalities, the more I learned about myself. One of the benefits of formal education is a stable, structured environment where we can discover personalities. You likely already know a little about your own personality, but there may be much more to discover. In this chapter, you're going to see how your personality can be a tool for guiding you into a well-suited career and fulfilling your God-given purpose.

Through this assessment exercise, you will discover how you get energized, take in information, make decisions, and structure your world. You'll see some careers that might fit your personality.

First, a quick overview: There are four basic personality types, and we are all a combination of these types. One type may be more dominant, but we all have a blend—a recipe, if you will—of the four personalities. Plenty of assessments are available to give you an idea your personality style.

My preferred and scientifically validated personality assessment is the Myers-Briggs Type Indicator. I use this assessment in almost all of my leadership development and student support work. You may wish to seek a certified MBTI practitioner to assist you with a formal Myers-Briggs personality assessment. Qualified practitioners exist in education, business, or career counseling centers. Your own workplace or someone in your network may offer this assessment.

Also, I can suggest (with caution) the following free option to test your personality type. There is a simple assessment at **16personalities.com**. However, the free version does not include the guidance of a certified practitioner. My intention is to provide options so that you can make your own choice.

◁ **Knowing your personality preferences helps you find what energizes you.** ▷

Knowing your personality preferences helps you find what energizes you and assists you in finding the best fit for your future choices. The Myers-Briggs assessment expresses your personality as four dichotomies: Extrovert/Introvert, Sensing/Intuition, Thinking/Feeling, and Judging/Perceiving. After you take the test, you learn to express your personality type in a four-letter code.

Here is a quick review of the characteristics used in the assessment exercise.

Extrovert/Introvert

The Extrovert/Introvert scale refers to the way your internal energy is charged. If you're an extrovert, you probably get energized by being with and around people. This is largely because extroverts process their thinking out loud with others. To be alone for long periods of time leaves an extrovert feeling drained and closed off from the world.

If you're a introvert, however, you may need alone time to recharge your batteries after you have been with or around people for long periods of time. Introverts like thinking inside their own minds and processing their thoughts without distractions; it brings them energy!

All of the personality preferences are equally important—none are better than the others. This is true for all the letters. How you are created, with the exact combination of letters, factors into your unique purpose.

◁ **All of the personality preferences are equally important —none are better than the others.** ▷

Sensing/Intuition

The Sensing/Intuition scale describes how you take in and process information. If you're a sensing person, you most likely take in information with your senses—sound, sight, taste, smell, touch—and you probably have a knack for details. Sensing personalities are anchored in the present.

Our intuitive friends (abbreviated with "N") are people who take in information through undefinable cues in the form of hunches and are "big-picture" focused. Intuitive personalities notice connections and patterns and are very future-oriented.

Thinking/Feeling

The Thinking/Feeling relationship describes the different ways that people make decisions. If you are a Thinker, you most likely are logical, factual, and very objective. Like journalist characters on TV shows from way back, you might hear a T say, "Just the facts, ma'am."

On the other hand, if you are a Feeler, you make decisions based on relationships and impact on people. Empathy is often a main driver for your decisions.

Judging/Perceiving

The last category, Judging/Perceiving, refers to the way you order your world. If you are a Judger, it's not a bad thing. It doesn't refer to being judgmental, but rather how you organize your preferences. You might be a quick decision-maker, valuing order and organization. You might prefer to make lists and check off what you accomplish. You may like things in their very organized place. If you accomplish something that is not on your list, you will probably add it just to check it off!

If you are a Perceiver, you tend to be open and flexible, and may not make decisions quickly so you can keep your options open. Ps are typically ready to try a new idea. Sometimes Ps can look like they are not completing things and that deadlines are not important, but they are really just in a designing or thinking process, exploring various options, with the final accomplishment still coming at the end, just in the nick of time.

Again, all the letters are valuable. Just because you have one letter in a category doesn't mean you never do something characteristic of the other letter in that category. Remember, we all have some level of all the letters. Some are just stronger preferences for your personality. All your letters are clues to how you are uniquely gifted toward some careers or ministries. Your four-letter personality type is another clue to your individual calling and purpose.

◁ Your four-letter personality type is another clue to your individual calling and purpose. ▷

Let the Dreaming Begin

If you haven't taken the personality assessment, here's your point of no return—go take it now, becuase the next Checkpoint uses your four-letter personality type.

Now, take a look at the several different combinations of these letters. In the "Resources" section of this book you will find a list of the careers that typically work well with each personality type. Take your four-letter combination and find it on that list. It's okay to dream a little bit. Look around at all of the careers and personality types. It's okay if you see careers that interest you in the other types. You will learn more as we go; we are just beginning.

If you see a few careers that pique your interest, find someone already doing that to talk to. Ask them about their job and their personality type. Perhaps you could explore volunteer or internship opportunities to try out these careers for yourself. Keep exploring to find what God has purposefully and plan-fully prepared for you! This exploration will be life-long as you grow, mature, and practice. You will develop skills, style and what is important to you. You will learn how your talents can be used and increased over time.

But you gotta start somewhere!

The main idea is to find a career or ministry with a combination of tasks that best uses your talents and personality style—that will energize you and not drain you.

What are your personality type assessment letters? To assist you, here are the possible examples of your four letters:

- The first letter will be **E** or **I**
- The second letter will be **S** or **N**
- The third letter will be **T** or **F**
- The fourth letter will be **J** or **P**

Place your letters in each of the four boxes below.

Now refer to "Careers with Your Personality Type" in the "Resources" section at the back of the book. You'll find sixteen lists that give careers to match your personality type preferences. In addition to your own list, you may also wish to explore the other personality lists for ideas. As you think about whether a choice would match you, make a note of anything that energizes you.

◁ Checkpoint #2: Know Yourself ▷

Assessing your personality style (what might fit you)

How do you get your energy?

How do you prefer to take in information?

How do you like to structure your world/work/life?

3 Why Skills & Accomplishments Matter

LET'S TAKE A LOOK in the rear-view mirror for just a moment. You've completed checkpoints one and two! Excellent! You noted what others have said about you and the skills other people see in you. Then you discovered your personality type and explored how it impacts your energy, information processing, decision making, and how you order your world. You even peeked at some careers that might match your individual personality, taking note of what energized you most.

Now it's time to look at your past from a different perspective—not just through what others say about your skills, but how your skills are displayed through your accomplishments. You never know—God just might build on those accomplishments again someday, somehow.

Ten Things You Love About You

Your next task is to think about ten accomplishments you are proud of *from all aspects of your life*. It could be from school, home, ministry, work, volunteering, or with friends and family. These accomplishments can be large or small; the importance lies within how these accomplishments really mattered to you. These may be things that you received public recognition for or things you just felt really good about doing. It's not about what others might think. In this moment, it's about what you value and what brings you energy and excitement.

I know, you're probably thinking that ten is way too high of a number for this task. You're sure you will not be able to come up with ten accomplishments. But you can. You have ten—even if you don't think you do.

And just when you were warming up to the number ten, let's add another dimension to this task: Two of the ten must have been achieved before you turned 15 years old. At 15, you weren't driving yet and your world was still restricted. So this is the time you were dreaming, wishing, and thinking about growing up. Your resources were limited, but as you were thinking and dreaming about your future, you were accomplishing things that were building blocks to your future career, ministry or service.

"For with God nothing shall be impossible."
—*Luke 1:37 (KJV)*

You may be thinking this is even more impossible than before. But that's not true. C'mon, you can do this! It's important for you to think and feel a little deeper—and this is a safe place for you to do that.

Remember, these ten accomplishments can be from any part of your life: school, volunteer work, paid work, ministry, family, etc. *(Hint: we are looking for patterns.)*

If you can't think of these accomplishments right away, that's okay. Don't hurry this task; pray for God to help you remember what has brought you joy and a sense of value in your life. Memories will begin to surface. Try this: Start a small notebook or a list on your phone. Carry it with you throughout the day, and keep it near you while you do your best thinking. Start building your accomplishment list one day at a time. An important part of this process is reflection—deep thinking—on what you have accomplished over time. Why was it meaningful, important to you? This is the key to finding the significance of these accomplishments.

Once you have your list of ten accomplishments, look at each event or accomplishment with a sense of deep satisfaction. Look at all the cool things you've done! Identify the skills or natural talents each accomplishment required.

How did each accomplishment energize you?

Look for patterns of skills within the accomplishments. Which one are you most proud of? Put an asterisk next to those ones.

Think about *why you are proud* of each of your accomplishments. Why? Because in my work as a career coach, I've found that looking for *patterns of skills* and values in all areas of life leads to what you do well—to your unique purpose.

Where you see similar tasks and repeated successes that you really enjoyed doing, those are actually clues to your unique purpose. Why these accomplishments mean something to you will point to potentially fulfilling careers and ministry.

Your skills are *what* you can do and what you are often naturally good at. They're what come easily to you and bring you a sense of joy or fulfillment. Your accomplishments and pride in each of them reveals your *why.* Your values and meaning of what is uniquely important to you is *why* you like doing them and help you know what to pursue in your career. God already gave you passion; He is showing you the skills He built within you by what you've already accomplished.

For example, some of my accomplishments from before I was 15 include: I was in school, county, and state-level spelling bees and came in second place in the state when I was 10 years old! When I was 11, I was selected to work in the principal's office as an office support aide, where I delivered materials to classrooms and helped with filing. I even

◁ **WHY?** ▷

reasons you are proud of accomplishments:

proudly wore a "safety girl" patch on my arm! I also taught myself to quilt when I was just 13.

Here's how all that ties together: I've worked in corporate human resources, organizational development, and leadership development training, which require a lot of communication and presentations. I learned a lot about color and design from my quilting hobby and that transferred to skills for designing colorful and catchy presentations, communications, and trainings.

I've successfully managed programs partly due to my experience in the principal's office. And I'm writing this book because I learned to spell well!

I've certainly built on those skills—I can spell more words now than I could when I was 10. But I could see the seed of that skill and enjoyment starting at a young age. Get the idea? All that you do, that you enjoy and use again and again in new and different ways—it's is all interconnected!

If it is easy, it is a skill!

Once you complete your list of accomplishments, share it with a trusted friend, coach, or mentor. Spend time reliving the stories of these meaningful successes and listen to yourself as you tell them. (By the way, this is practice for interviewing. Keep that in the back of your mind for later!) Ask your trusted friend to give you feedback. Perhaps they will hear something and give you some new ideas to help you see yourself and your unique purpose in new ways.

ProTip: Interview Strategy

When you seek a career or ministry position, you'll go to interviews where you'll have to sell your skills. Doing this exercise of recording your skills and previous accomplishments will help you see God's developing purpose for your life.

So this is not an impossible mission, but one that is uniquely yours to discover. I can't do this one for you. You will often face missions that seem impossible. But, as Luke 1:37 says, "For with God nothing shall be impossible" (KJV). God gave me this verse when I was 15 and it has stuck with me ever since. Now I want to encourage you with it. Through Him, we can accomplish much more than we could ever imagine.

Okay, go get started on your list—I know you can do it!

◁ Checkpoint #3: Ten Accomplishments ▷

List ten things you love about you. (Remember to think of a few before age 15!)

1.
2.
3.
4.
5.
6.
7.
8.
9.
10.

What about these accomplishments meant so much to you?

Do you see any repeated patterns of skills or talents in your list?

Which of these skills and talents matter most to you? Why? How are you still using them in some way?

Look back at your list of accomplishments and think about the people who were with you or watched you succeed in these things. Talk to them (if possible) and get their perspective on your accomplishments and skills.

What skills, talents, or natural abilities did they see or hear in you through these accomplishments?

What patterns stood out to them?

How have you made a difference in their life or in someone else's life through your accomplishments?

Hint: *Maybe you motivated people to try harder; you advocated for someone else; your belief in someone made a difference; you taught someone something; you created something new; you fixed something tangible (like a car or bike) or some abstract thing (like a process or a program); you raised money; you led a team, etc.*

4 Values: Your Energy Motivators

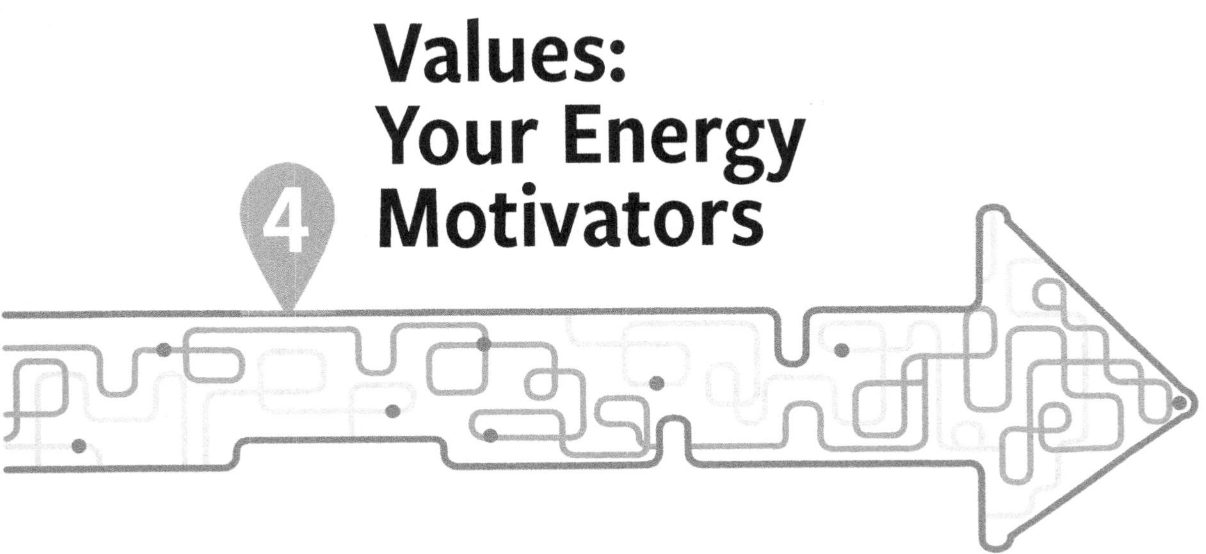

YOUR DOG MIGHT be sleeping on the floor, out cold, maybe even dreaming. But when you say, "Do you wanna go for a walk?" he probably perks right up. He might even get up off the floor and trot over to the door. Maybe he tilts his head and waits for you to hook up his leash. Why? Because he values walking with you, and suddenly he's got all the energy in the world. He didn't even need any coffee! A walk, something he values, is an energy motivator.

Identify your values by asking what gives you energy. You might not get excited about going for a walk, but there are other things in your life that motivate and jump-start your energy! Don't worry—you can still have coffee.

What Are Your Values?

Values are the drivers of your life. Your values are something that energizes you, and they are what you are willing to stand for because of a deep conviction. Values are within you. They are the internal force that drives you toward work or ministry, and they'll be the conduit for you to make a difference in the world.

They also help keep balance in your life and help you stay focused on what is most important to you.

I once had a leader in my life who had no qualms about acting less than kind toward those in lower positions. I often found myself standing in the gap for those mistreated employees as a mediator between this leader and those who justifiably feared the leader. You see, I discovered I would stand strong as an advocate for those who were afraid. Advocacy is still a strong value of mine. It combines with another value that I hold dear—*fairness*, the equitable treatment of others no matter their level or walk of life.

Conversely, a value can be something that gives you positive creative energy. For me, creativity is one of my strongest values. It means being able to design something new or something that has never been done before. For me, it might be a training, a beautiful quilt, a new presentation, or a renovation for my home to bring me comfort. Creativity and design provide high levels of energy and satisfaction.

◁ **Values define how we feel and think about what is most important to us.** ▷

Why? Because I can bring new learning to the people I coach and train and can help them change, find new strengths, and new ways of thinking to better their lives.

I also value comfort and efficiency, so I have custom-designed ways to conserve space (built in collaboration with my contractor husband), while making a room to support others with a safe and comfy environment. I used my values to create an environment where people can thrive or rest. My library has become my grandchildren's quiet place to hang out and have peace away from their siblings!

Values Matter

What value is so important to you that you would stand to defend it? What value is something you can't live without because it gives you so much energy and joy? Values define how we feel and think about what is most important to us—we might even fight for it if needed.

Speaking of fighting for something—a special thanks to all of our armed forces personnel who serve and sometimes have to fight to maintain our country's freedom, and for the difference they make in our lives with their values of advocacy for freedom. As some of you finish your service, this book is also for you!

I want you to think about what *really matters to you in your life*. Notice I said your *life* and not just your *work*. Your life purpose to serve is based on who you are and not just on what you do. We talked about that a little bit in chapter one, but here's where we really get to dig into what that means.

◁ **VALUES** ▷
start to list what really matters in your life:

In my work as a coach in human resources and organizational leadership departments, I've discovered something interesting about humanity. A huge part of my role was helping to settle disputes. Not the most fun part of my job, but somehow we always worked through it and came out okay in the end. But one thing I noticed: over 90% of the tussles I assisted in untangling revolved around one thing: Values.

Values are the non-negotiable, important standards that really matter to you. Values are what you live your life by. Your values matter so much to you that you would not let anyone take them away from you. You would fight for them if you felt someone was asking you to give them up.

In order to serve others and find your best fit—and perhaps reduce the conflicts you may encounter in your work and life—you must know and hold onto your values. This will help you make better choices that support your God-given values. This is true for finding your best fit for work, but also choosing your friends, your spouse, and making other important values-based choices in your life.

God expects us to hold fast to our faith, and He tells us to stand for Him. Your faith is one of your most basic God-given values.

◁ Checkpoint 4: Your Most Important Values ▷

To get started, here are some examples of values. Use these to help you make your own top-ten list.

Values—sample list

Achievement
Adventure
Advocacy
Affiliation
Artistic Creativity
Change
Close to Power
Collaboration
Competition
Decision Making

Ethics
Fame
Family
Fast Pace
Friendship
Helping Society
High Earnings
Hospitality
Influence
Job Tranquility
Knowledge

Leadership
Leisure
Location
Mediation
Nurturing Others
Order
Physical Exercise
Power
Problem Solving
Public Contact
Respect

Stability
Status/Prestige
Strategy
Support
Time Freedom
Variety
Working Alone
Working with Data
Working with People
Working with Tools

Reflect on the list above and add any words you think should be included. Adding words doesn't necessarily mean that you must choose them as a value. We are brainstorming!

Okay, now it's time to make your list of values.

- Think about why you chose a certain job or volunteer position in the past.
- Think about why you *didn't* choose to participate in a certain activity or job or volunteer position.

You likely chose something because *it appealed to one of your values.* And on the flip side, you likely chose not to do something because it *went against your values* strongly enough for you to decide not to participate in the activity or accept the job.

Exercise on next page: List at least ten of your values. Next, rank them in order from one to ten, with one being the most important to you and ten being the least important (the easiest for you to live without). To be fair, this exercise is one of the hardest, but it's also one of the most valuable! You can think about this one over a span of time instead of all at once. Ask for God's help! (Matthew 7:7)

My Top Ten Values

1. ....
2. ....
3. ....
4. ....
5. ....
6. ....
7. ....
8. ....
9. ....
10. ....

Once you've completed your list, talk it over with someone you trust—a coach, mentor, or friend. They may see some things in you that you don't yet see in yourself.

Take time to reflect and really see yourself as God does. By slowing down to think and feel deeply, you can unlock things about yourself—like finding precious memories in the attic, trunks storing and preserving what is most important to you. What might you find when you open those dusty trunks in the recesses of your heart and mind? It will help you remember who made you, to whom you belong, and what brings you joy.

These values—and your skills—make up who you are. And as you put these pieces together, you'll feel the warmth of the comforting quilt you're creating with the fragments of your life.

Going Deeper

What about these top-ten values you listed make them so meaningful and important to you? Why?

Now here's the hard part: *If you could only have five of them,* which five would you choose? Would it change your ranking of your top five? How would you re-rank them?

1. ______
2. ______
3. ______
4. ______
5. ______

Why did you choose these five values? Why did you choose them over the other five?

Think of a time when you used at least two of these values in a situation, and you were proud of the outcome. What skills, talents, style, and knacks did you also use in this situation?

As you remember and reflect, what does all this mean to you?

5 Your Unique Blueprint

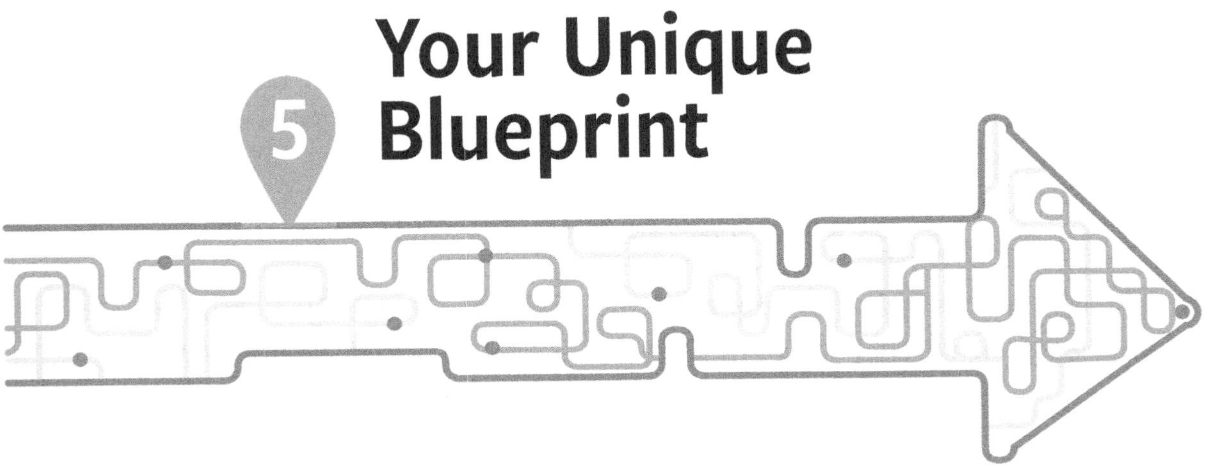

ODDLY ENOUGH, I've worked my entire career with senior leaders, but I've never actually been a senior leader. I cannot explain this except for God's hand in my life and career.

My unique characteristic is that I have a unique way of building trust with senior leaders—high level, highly educated people—and make deep connections with them in a relatively short time frame. I can see connections with what seems like random or seemingly unlike things, and somehow that connects with something in that leader to quickly create trust.

One example is my friend Bob. He was a senior leader with whom I built trust quickly, and our friendship lasted twenty years after we stopped working together.

Are you Unique? Yes! God says so!

Since you've already learned so much about yourself—your personality, natural skills, your values, let's see what God has to say about your uniqueness.

In Psalm 139, God says you are knitted together in the womb by God, "fearfully and wonderfully made." Joshua 1:5 says, "Before I formed you in the womb, I knew you."

Each person is created uniquely. Let's look at these fascinating facets in your God-given, diamond-shaped, brilliantly-lit life.

> "For we are God's handiwork, created in Christ Jesus to do good works, which God prepared in advance for us to do."
>
> *—Ephesians 2:10*

You have a unique, physical, organic blueprint—demonstrated by DNA and fingerprints—as well as a unique personality, skillset, and God-given values. In order to best serve and bring glory to God, you must look for this uniqueness in how God created you. Remember, He says you're a masterpiece!

"For we are God's handiwork, created in Christ Jesus to do good works, which God prepared in advance for us to do" (Ephesians 2:10). Other versions of that verse use the word *masterpiece* or *workmanship* instead of "handiwork."

So, how are you unique? What knacks or abilities do you have? It could be with people, information, or tools. Even your quirks are intentionally part of you, too! I have some very practical unique skills but also some quirky ones. Together, they all make me into the person God can use for specific things.

For example: I see faces, expressions, and even emotions in the front of cars and inanimate objects. I see happy, sad, grumpy, elegant, even perky faces! I buy a car based partly on the expression on its face and the emotions it seems to project. Kind of like the movie *Cars*. Weird, right? I know. But let me break this down and show you how quirks can be powerful and purposeful.

I came to realize it takes real creativity to see cars and other objects in this way. It also demonstrates something else that is very strong in me: I am relational. I'm always seeking those happy faces as the fun-loving person I try to be. It also represents my love of coaching and counseling and my spiritual gift of encouragement. I am always super aware of moods and when people might need encouragement.

Sure, it's quirky! And yet, it's a representation of the helping and teaching skills I love to use. This unusual way of thinking also helps me see word pictures and make connections to symbolic stories and metaphors that have hidden meaning. Jesus used these in the parables He told. (And the Bible even talks about cars! After all, it says all the disciples "came together in one accord." Isn't that a Honda? Ha! Okay, I know it's a bad joke. Forgive me! Just my quirky, creative, fun thinking at play again.)

This quirk of mine happens so often, people frequently tell me they would have never thought of it that way. I'm gratified by this statement because as a trainer and coach, teaching others to see from a different and new perspective is very important to me.

In fact, one of my favorite quotes is from Alexandra K. Trenfor: "The best teachers tell you where to look, but not what to see."

◁**The best teachers tell you where to look, but not what to see.**▷
—Alexandra K. Trenfor

Like the faces in cars, I am attempting to show you a new way to see things. And through this book I'm trying to show you yourself—kind of like a mirror—but not tell you what to see or give you all the answers. The answers are within you and between you and your Creator, God.

Embrace Your Quirks

You might not see faces in cars like I do, but can you think of something in your life that is maybe a bit quirky, but helps you think or see differently than everyone else? That's not a bad thing! Different thinking can help you identify skills and passions. When you look beyond the surface of a quirk, you might find deeper meanings in yourself that you've never thought about before.

You'll complete your next checkpoint by thinking about some natural—and maybe even quirky—things you do that others have noticed and maybe even commented on.

Let me give you a less silly example from my CareerMap.

I've been told I'm extremely fast at processing information to grasp the big picture and see where it fits in the future. I see possibilities and connections in a fraction of the time others take to get to the same place. This translates into natural influencing, leadership, decision-making skills and strategizing any future plans needed.

This unique trait is a two-edged sword; I often have to work to exercise my patience with others as they catch up with my thoughts and ideas.

This creative thinking ability, coupled with my quirky way of seeing things, allows me to lead discussions and design and facilitate workshops. People often comment on the *wow* feeling they get as they see things from a very different point of view.

I said I have a knack for helping people see things from a different perspective. Seriously—will you ever look at the front of a car the same way again?

◁ Checkpoint #5: Embrace Your Quirks! ▷

You've listed your skills, your unique personality, your accomplishments, your values, and now it's time to see what makes you unique.

How do you see your world uniquely? Who or what types of people can you reach that no one else can? Or what can you fix like no one else around you? What parts or details of things are you able to see or show others? Or how can you help others from your big-picture view?

Stop and ask God to show you your uniqueness. He said you were uniquely made for His purposes. If you ask Him, He will begin to show you.

How are you unique or quirky? How do you see things or think about things differently? List three ways you are unique:

1. ______________________________
2. ______________________________
3. ______________________________

How do you feel about those things? Why?

What did you discover about yourself during this thinking and feeling process?

How could you use this awareness in seeking what God has for you in your future, or even right now?

6 The Kaleidoscope of You

I'VE ALWAYS LOVED kaleidoscopes! I even received one as a gift not long ago. I love how the bright images shift into a totally different pattern with just one small turn. It's fascinating to see how different the patterns could become.

Like a kaleidoscope, you are a person of many facets. You've seen this more clearly through the various checkpoints, and I hope you are realizing how unique and wonderfully made you are.

You have accomplished and enjoyed many experiences, both paid and volunteer, as a test drive to see if they fit. Keep in mind that skills gained in volunteering experiences are as important as paid employment. Another important outcome of volunteering your skills and connections is called net-giving, which is another word for servant leadership. It's a skill that shows you care about others' welfare and success as much as you do your own. Net-giving also brings relationships into your life which can lead to many new opportunities.

Perhaps an even better example of this servant leadership thinking is how Jesus modeled caring for others as well in the Bible.

ProTip: Net-giving

The idea of net-giving is from one of my favorite authors, Tommy Spaulding, who wrote *It's Not Just Who You Know,* a book that you should read. Tommy is a committed leadership development expert.

Many of the volunteer net-giving activities I do lead to someone trusting me and then asking me to train, coach, or speak. In fact, I've had eight different jobs created for me from leaders who heard me speak, watched me train or care for someone else. When others see you doing something you do well because you love it, they often want to share in it. That is how unselfish service works. It also helps to hone your skills as you practice them.

"Give, and it will be given to you. A good measure, pressed down, shaken together and running over, will be poured into your lap. For with the measure you use, it will be measured to you" (Luke 6:38).

"Give, and it will be given to you."
—Luke 6:38

The verse starts with "Give, and it will be given to you." But, caution: Don't give to get, but rather to serve God in what He is leading you to. He will bless you in the way it fits His plan. He will also use what you are about to discover—what He has already placed in your heart to do and how are you are equipped to do it with His help.

Energizing You

So, your next checkpoint explores what God has called you to do by answering these questions:

1. What kind of activities and tasks most charge your internal batteries?
2. What activities do you love to do so much you would do them even if no one paid you? (You would do these even if no one paid you because they trigger something passionate within you.)

If you're like me, you probably won't say that scrubbing toilets is something you'd like to do without a paycheck. But if you're someone who really enjoys making things clean for hospitality or helping people enjoy a clean environment, then maybe scrubbing toilets is something you consider an act of service. You'd even do it if you don't get paid because you're passionate about hospitality and taking care of others. It is the why of service that drives you to serve, not always service itself.

Okay, that's a weird example. But seriously, the answer to this question will help you discover your talents, skills, and passions as you grow in your purpose. God put desires in your heart and created you with innate talents for both your current and future actions.

I have strong empathy for those who lose their job. It is disorienting, scary, and sometimes feels hopeless. Some of my friends and I have experienced being downsized from our jobs in the past. As a result, in these shared painful times, we collaborated on how to help others get through painful experiences.

We partnered with others like us and created a career transition ministry consortium for those who lost their jobs within many local places of worship. We trained and coached a multitude of people over a period of ten years—and not one of us ever got a paycheck.

But realizing what I'd do even without a paycheck led to contacts for paid coaching later on. Why? Because some of my paying clients saw that I loved training and coaching so much that I would do it for free. I became more and more skilled, and it created paid opportunities in the long run.

What are those things you love to do that could lead you to your purpose?

If you're willing to engage in something without getting paid for it, you may love doing it, and you are probably good at it.

When you don't enjoy doing something, it's not usually what you prefer to do in your personal life, work, or

◁ **WORK** ▷

that you enjoy enough to do without getting paid:

____

____

____

____

____

volunteer work. If it doesn't energize you, it probably isn't a strength. Things that don't energize you drain you. Chances are you're not willing to volunteer for things that drain you. And you probably don't want to do those things even for a paycheck.

When you're good at something and you like to do it, you're already internally motivated.

However, when you're energized by doing something AND you're good at it, you're motivated by both external and internal rewards: excitement, energy, a feeling of satisfaction, and thinking you might wish to make this your life's work or ministry. You might find that you long to keep doing these activities just because you enjoy them.

Energy is also music to hiring leaders' ears! When little or no external motivation is needed, difficulties are reduced for both you and your leader. When you're working within your most energizing kinds of activities, you'll be self-directed and even become an influencer or leader!

This also makes you a human resources leader or a hiring manager's gold mine! If you're hired to do what you do well and enjoy, the hiring manager looks good to their leader, and that usually works out well for you as well. Trust me, I know—I was one of those HR leaders!

The most important reason is that you please God as He has uniquely wired you with talents you love to guide you on your career journey.

The Biblical Perspective

The Parable of the Talents (Matthew 25:14–30) tells the story of a master giving different amount of talents to each of his three servants. The *talents* are actually sums of money. (I think God used that word so we would make the direct connection to how we use our skills and abilities as currency and not just money).

The master gave each servant a different sum of money

or talents and expected each servant to use his talents to do the master's work, to multiply what He gave them. Two of the three did just that, but the third one buried the money in the ground. He didn't even use it. When the master returned, he was disappointed by the buried talents and didn't give that servant anything else to be responsible for.

The master replied to the man whom he gave the five talents, "Well done, good and faithful servant! You have been faithful with a few things; I will put you in charge of many things. Come and share your master's happiness!" (Matthew 25:21).

The parallel to your talents—your skills, gifts, and abilities—is unmistakable. Your talents are the things you do with ease, that energize you, that you hone and increase through learning and using them. We each have different and unique talents to develop and use for God's work. And as you use the things God's gifted you with, you'll feel God's pleasure—your master's happiness. You might even get more responsibilities and opportunities to accomplish great things for Him!

You are unique—one of a kind—as evidenced by your fingerprints and in your unique DNA. God has created you for a work that only you can do. Ephesians 2:10 says, "For we are God's handiwork, created in Christ Jesus to do good works, which God prepared in advance for us to do."

Before you get skeptical or have self-doubt, remember what we already saw in Matthew 25. God gives specific talents and expects us to use them. And in Ephesians 2:10, we see that there's work for us to do already prepared by God!

Doesn't that inspire you—to know that you are part of God's customized plan?

God has given clues all around you about how He made you and His purpose for your life. Think about the skills in the fun things you do, and you will begin to see a pattern in this kaleidoscope of sparkling clues from the joys in your life.

Don't Believe the Lies

Even now, you may hear a voice that says you do not have any talents or skills! But that's a lie from the enemy. He doesn't want you to do God's will, or to co-partner with God in His plan, or to have that abundant life Jesus promises:

"The thief comes only to steal and kill and destroy; I have come that they might have life, and have it to the full" (John 10:10).

> "In the same way, let your light shine before others, that they may see your good deeds and glorify your Father in heaven."
> —Matthew 5:16

Because you have an enemy—the thief—you must dismiss those lies, as those can create internal barriers that can keep you from finding your purpose. In the next chapter, we'll identify how, in faith and through trusting God, you can overcome these barriers.

For this part of our work, I encourage you to focus on believing God's truth and ignoring the lies. You are made for a purpose and you do have God-given skills. God has promised you unique talents and gifts to do His work. Through Him you are successful—not in your own strength, but as servants through Him. His mission is to bring Jesus' love to others by bringing more love, service, kindness, and meaning to the world. When you do good things because of Jesus—when you use your talents—you bring honor to the Creator.

"In the same way, let your light shine before others, that they may see your good deeds and glorify your Father in heaven" (Matthew 5:16).

Believe in God and in yourself! He created you, your talents, your work, your passion, and your joy. You can own your strengths and uniqueness, and yet God is the author of your strengths and uniqueness in His plan for you.

What Charges Your Batteries?

You've already listed some skills you know you're good at. But now let's look at the skills and talents you love doing. What are the activities and tasks that charge your batteries? Here are some ideas to get you started:

◁ **ASSIGNMENT** ▷
Make a check mark next to the activities and tasks that charge your batteries.

- o Do people often seek you out for wise counsel? Do you enjoy listening and helping them solve their problems? Do you walk with them in their hurts and joys?
- o Do you possess a natural mechanical ability? Do you like to take things apart and tinker with motors or electronics and experiment with gizmos? Do you adjust and fix things easily? Do you like to build things with your hands?
- o Do you find yourself researching? On the internet, through talking with people, reading books or articles? Do you enjoy investigating new ways of doing things, finding new information, or studying something for long periods of time?
- o Do you spend time looking at the stars or being in nature? Do you enjoy using chemical combinations, discovering how natural things are made, investigating wildlife, going hunting or fishing, or even examining bugs?
- o Do you like to do hands-on activities like construction, architecture, gardening, or farming? Do you enjoy working with animals or other living things?
- o Do you enjoy taking care of people? Serving food, reading to the sick, elderly, or children? Hosting dinner parties in your home, or organizational events, or group activities?
- o Do you enjoy making your home environmentally friendly? Do you like to recycle, create new ways to be energy efficient, or otherwise care for the environment?
- o Do you like being creative? Designing things? Drawing,

painting, sewing, home decorating, quilting, making clothes, crafting, scrapbooking, woodworking, crocheting, or knitting?

Or something else entirely? Now think about your favorite part of your daily routine. Which activities do you enjoy doing? Which do you not enjoy or even hate doing? What do you like to do on the weekends or in your free time?

About now you're probably saying, "What is so important about these everyday activities?"

Everything!

When you get excited about an everyday thing, that's a clue to what's in your heart. What are your passions? What do you truly enjoy?

Once you answer that, the next step is determining the skills required for doing those things and continuing to improve them. This builds your skills, and you increase your influence with others.

However, there might be aspects of a certain activity that you don't enjoy—that's okay. I love to make quilts. I love designing the patterns, the color selections, and the finished quilt. But I am not all that crazy about the long time it takes to sew it.

Overall, notice what kinds of activities pique your interest and give you energy or a boost of satisfaction. These are your battery chargers.

◁ Checkpoint #6: Your Battery Chargers ▷

Are there any activities in the "What Charges Your Batteries?" list above that you noticed about your energy? Did one or two of them spark something in your heart? Circle or mark an asterisk by those ones. Now it's your turn to make your own list!

List three to five activities that energize you and you absolutely love doing. Remember, these are things you might even do without a paycheck.

1. ....
2. ....
3. ....
4. ....
5. ....

Now think about what skills you might need for these activities. For example: If you really love fixing things like cars or other machines, a required skill would be knowing how to operate a variety of tools. Or if you love researching, you'd need to know how to use online databases and the library search tools and even new software being developed for research.

List at least one skill required for each of the activities you mentioned above.

1. ....
2. ....
3. ....
4. ....
5. ....

Look back at your list of enjoyable activities. What are your thoughts or feelings about those activities?

Which one are you most excited about?

Why is that?

What are some things that you think you might be interested in, but you've never tried?

What steps would you need to take to start trying those things?

7 Busting Internal Barriers

"'My grace is sufficient for you, for my power is made perfect in weakness.'"—2 Corinthians 12:9

"The only limit to our realization of tomorrow will be our doubts of today. Let us move forward with strong and active faith."—Franklin D. Roosevelt

LIKE THE kaleidoscope we talked about earlier, you've discovered a beautiful collage of vibrant color and patterns as you've put together all your skills, talents, and gifts. You've realized new things about yourself, or perhaps you've seen yourself in a different way. You've identified the ways you are unique, what you value, and what brings you energy.

And with all these things and the ideas you're recording here in this book, you have a rich resource! You're packing these things in your suitcase, and it's the best of who you are all in one place.

Be encouraged—God used awesome creative energy to make you a person who will accomplish great things for Him. He designed you and built you, and He's planning to do great things through you.

There is one bit of bad news, though. I don't like talking about it, but we have to. There is an enemy that wants to keep you from what you are meant to do. He doesn't want you to know, explore, or understand your God-given purpose. And he definitely doesn't want you to actually fulfill your purpose. So he uses internal barriers in your life—those weaknesses we hate in ourselves—to keep you from that success.

Internal barriers are those nagging habits that distract you from God's plan for your life. Like your God-given strengths, these barriers can follow you from career to career and can often hinder your success in work, your personal life, and relationships—if you let them.

But according to God, we are overcomers. Romans 8:37 says, ". . . In all these things we are more than conquerors through him who loved us."

"In all these things we are more than conquerors through him who loved us."

—Romans 8:37

You can have victory over your internal barriers. God can use your weaknesses as long as you keep taking them back to Him and talking with Him about them. Have courage—we all have internal barriers, and we can overcome them with God's help.

These internal barriers will tag along as stowaways in your suitcase, and they will try to always take over or jump out to steal the show whenever they can. They're annoying, to be sure, but you can wrangle them, tame them, and eventually work them to your advantage. But first you must identify them.

The next page lists some internal barriers or struggles you might recognize in yourself.

Internal Barriers—Sample list

- Abrasiveness
- Absentmindedness
- Avoiding conflict
- Being a show-off
- Being thin-skinned
- Being withdrawn
- Being inconsiderate
- Critical
- Competitiveness
- Complaining
- Controlling
- Condemning
- Cynicism
- Defensiveness
- Fear/Terror
- Harsh tone
- Laziness
- Obsessive tendencies
- Pride
- Selfishness
- Self-hate
- Self-pity
- Self-sabotaging
- Short-tempered
- Should or ought-to thinking
- Suspicious of others' motives
- Tight control over emotions
- Uneasy about appearance
- Unrealistic expectations
- Ungratefulness
- Vulnerable to real or imagined threats
- Workaholism
- Worry
- **The Enemy's Lies:**
  - o God can't use me
  - o I am too young
  - o I am too old
  - o I am not skilled
  - o I am not enough

Notice that many of these barriers may start out as good traits. For example, workaholism may start out as a good work ethic and a drive to succeed. Cynicism may start out as a well-used set of critical thinking skills. Control could begin as protecting a value, but could lead to commanding, domineering, and not considering others. Avoiding conflict starts out as a desire to not cause or stir up trouble, but it also could turn into an unwillingness to work through a situation. Laziness may come from a laid-back personality.

Many internal barriers are a character or personality trait taken too far in the wrong direction.

That's where the enemy likes to play. He wants to take you in the wrong direction because then you won't be doing what God designed you for. Yes, you read that right: God even designs our weakness so we will learn, grow, and depend on Him. The enemy wants to keep you as far from your purpose as possible.

So here's the thing. You can't just identify these barriers and then ignore them. It doesn't work to simply acknowledge them and then let them be. Ignoring them just won't cut it. You have to actively fight them and sometimes rely on God and on others' strengths to overcome them.

I want to stop here and say one thing before we move on. I don't want you to read this list and say, "Wow, I struggle with a lot of those barriers. I must be an awful person and I won't be able to do anything right. I might as well not even try."

That's not the message I want you to hear at all. That's how the enemy wants you to read this chapter, but not how God wants you to read it.

Here's the real truth: We are all human, and we all have flaws. You aren't perfect. If you think you are, then you may have some more soul searching to do. God created you for good works, and He gives you the power to do those good works and resources to overcome your internal barriers in order to accomplish His purpose for your life. God declares you an overcomer!

Overcoming: Make a Plan

◁ **I often tell myself to *do it afraid*, to challenge myself to risk the rejection.** ▷

We already know we can't just identify and get comfortable with these barriers. We can't just name them and then ignore them. That's not how overcoming works.

If you are dealing with internal barriers, they're probably hindering you and need to be reduced as much as possible. You need an action plan.

My action plan to overcome the fear of rejection was to try to talk to people that are difficult to talk with, like high-level leaders who aren't easily approachable. This forced me out of my comfort zone. I often tell myself to *do it afraid*, to challenge myself to risk the rejection, thus lessening the power of that barrier a little bit each time. I also researched rejection and found action strategies that an encourager, who is on my personal board of directors, holds me accountable for. I knew if I gave in to my fear of rejection, I would never be able to train and coach people or build strong relationships at work, home, or church.

I search for and memorize Bible verses about Jesus' love for me and how He will never reject me. Scripture and prayer are our first line of defense! (Read Joshua 1:9, Isaiah 41:10, and John 10:10.)

Your action plan might also include seeking out an encouraging friend who will keep you accountable and pray for you. It may include you putting some steady, specific prayer time in for these barriers. And practicing skills that counteract these weaknesses is another strategy that must be in your action plan. Wise counsel and confirmation from others can be a second defense against the enemy!

God says you are an overcomer (Romans 8:37). He will help you overcome your internal barriers. God often allows weaknesses so we will keep running back to Him and His strength. You may never completely rid yourself of these weaknesses. You may always have a natural tendency toward one or two. Second Corinthians 12:9 says, "My grace is sufficient for you, for my power is made perfect in weakness. Therefore I will boast all the more gladly about my weaknesses, so that Christ's power may rest on me."

"In all these things we are more than conquerors through him who loved us."
—*Romans 8:37*

God, in His timing and strength, will help you accomplish His purpose for your life despite your barriers. Having an action plan, an encouraging friend, and a graceful God who says, "My strength is made perfect in weakness" will help you make progress. He'll help you respond to those tendencies and temptations, and each time you do, it will be easier and easier to recognize and resist them.

Sometimes God allows the weaknesses so He will be made known in the good things you do. Sometimes our weaknesses and barriers are there so the work we do can glorify God, not ourselves. He helps us accomplish our purpose, and many times we couldn't do those things without

Him. Sometimes those barriers can help remind us who we are in Jesus.

◁ I search for and memorize Bible verses about Jesus' love for me and how He will never reject me. ▷

Even the apostle Paul said he did the things he wished he didn't do and struggled to do the things he knew he should do (see Romans 7). We are in good company as human beings. We all have something we must work on to be successful in God's plan for our lives.

Start building your action plan so you are ready when the enemy strikes with those internal barriers. How will you overcome those barriers and potential roadblocks to God's purpose for your life? Remember all the strengths you've discovered thus far. Remind yourself that you are created by God for a specific purpose; He just might use that weakness as a way to encourage someone else.

◁ Checkpoint #7: Identify Your Internal Barriers ▷

What internal barriers can you identify in your life?

Which ones present the biggest battle for you? Why do you think that is?

Which ones scare you the most? Why?

What are some actions you can take to start overcoming these barriers? Be specific.

Who are some wise friends you could ask to help you overcome your barriers?

Ask God today to help you identify barriers. Ask Him to help you overcome them. Ask Him to send you encouragers to come alongside and help you overcome these barriers. Ask Him to show you ways that you can reach others through your weaknesses.

8 You—on Purpose

"Everything is possible for one who believes."—Mark 9:23

"Commit to the LORD whatever you do,
and he will establish your plans."—Proverbs 16:3

TAKE A LOOK at your suitcase. You've piled lots of really cool things in it! It will travel with you wherever you go throughout life. There's one really important thing we still need to drop in that suitcase, though. But first, let me tell you the story that inspired me for this last suitcase item.

One of my favorite Bible heroes is David. David loved God and put Him first, and then God chose him to be king. David became a man after God's own heart and ultimately served in his purpose.

You can read the whole story in I Samuel 17, but here's a bit of it:

The people wanted a human king like other kingdoms rather than only God as ruler. God allowed the people's request and permitted Samuel the prophet to anoint Saul to be king. He wasn't a very good king, and he disobeyed God, so when it came time to pick a successor, David came on the scene. Let's look at David's unique purpose.

God instructed Samuel, the priest, to go to Jesse's house to anoint the next king. Jesse had several sons, and David was one of them, but when Samuel got there, David wasn't even called in from the fields. His dad didn't think David, a small and rugged shepherd, was a likely candidate to be king. His brothers, on the other hand, were tall and powerful, and any of them would have been a shoo-in, a sure bet by human standards.

"Everything is possible for one who believes."
—Mark 9:23

David was handsome, sure, but he was the youngest and just didn't look like what the father thought a king should look like. David was finally called in after God passed on all of David's older, more kingly-looking brothers, at which point the priest asked if there were any other sons. David was finally called in, chosen, and commissioned as Israel's next king. But this was a future appointment, as Saul was still on the throne.

Not long after, David was left out in the fields with the sheep again while his brothers camped with the nation's army. They were fighting an enemy whose not-so-secret weapon was a giant named Goliath. They knew they couldn't win by size, strength, or numbers. Everyone was afraid of Goliath, and each day he would mock Israel, taunting them for their cowardice—including David's big and strong brothers.

When David arrived at the battlefield, not as a soldier but as a delivery boy for his brothers, he saw the giant and wondered why no one in Israel would fight to defend God's honor.

To David, it was simple, If you are a soldier for the living God, what is there to fear? He decided if no one else would fight then it would just have to be him. Besides, in his line of work as a shepherd, he'd killed a lion and a bear with his bare hands, and God saved him from both. He figured God would do the same with Goliath. (Faith is power!)

So David—the shepherd boy whose own father passed him over to be king because of his small stature—was going to fight a real giant. This hadn't been in David's plans that day; he hadn't brought anything with him, so King Saul offered his battle gear for David to wear. But, once he got everything on, he knew he couldn't use it. He had never used this type of gear before, and he didn't have time to practice with it. It would do nothing but encumber him in a fight.

Instead, David went down to the river and chose five smooth stones. His only weapon was a slingshot, but this was his skill. He was an expert shot; he had used it plenty of times to ward off threats to his flock. He knew his sling and how the stones would fly out of it. He selected each stone carefully, taking into account its weight, size, and texture—the smoother, the better. He knew the strength of his arm and how close he'd have to be to launch those stones and reach the target, Goliath.

He also knew he couldn't bear to hear the giant mocking God any more. He knew how to use his sling, and he came prepared with the stones. But David also knew God would be the one to help him slay the giant. His co-partnership with God was his real strength, and yet David was ready.

"Commit to the LORD whatever you do, and he will establish your plans." —Proverbs 16:3

You probably know the rest of the story. David, now facing the mocking giant, grabbed a stone from his bag, put it in his sling, and circled it over his head like he'd done hundreds of times before. The stone soared through the air and lodged in Goliath's forehead.

The giant, jolted by the flying stone to the forehead, teetered and fell face down on the ground. David, who wasn't carrying even a sword—only his sling, and he still had four stones left—ran over and took the giant's own sword to cut off his head, sealing Israel's victory over the Philistines.

Goliath was dead, and the Philistines, without their superstar warrior, were terrified. They turned and ran away.

David was small and weak compared to Goliath. But he depended totally on God to fight for him. He did what he knew—he was skilled in using his slingshot. But he trusted God to take care of the giant and God did. God promises to work in weakness.

You never know when God will call on you for a mission. Just think about the stories shared around David's family dinner table that night!

Read more stories from David's life and you'll see how God kept working through David's weaknesses. Not to mention the stories of Moses, Job, Samson, Gideon, and everyone in the Bible. God used external and internal barriers, strengths, and weaknesses to accomplish His purposes. Don't think it will be any different with you. God promises to work through your strengths and weaknesses, too.

Now that you have all this information about yourself and are beginning to understand who God has created you to become, through education, faith, personality, and experiences, you can dive deep into your purpose and mission.

Crafting Your Purpose Statement

David didn't have a formal purpose statement before he met Goliath, but he did have a clear mission. He had predetermined in his heart that he would stand for the living God.

David might not have had it written out—letterhead wasn't really a thing back then—but he had it written in his heart, and he did not waiver from it. He had lots of time to think about a purpose statement while he was out in the field with the sheep, at least when he wasn't killing a bear or a lion. He had etched it in his mind and heart.

And when the time came for him to act quickly, the time spent building his purpose statement came in handy. He was ready to move and act upon his predetermined purpose: to stand for the living God, no matter what.

You're probably not a shepherd spending hours, even days or weeks, by yourself with only sheep to talk to. You probably have a lot of other things flying through your mind all the time. Even this book is giving you plenty of things to think about. So you're going to need to set aside time to think specifically about your purpose statement.

Creating a personal purpose statement is an incredibly powerful task to connect what you stand for and what God will partner with you to do. The act of writing it down, finding the right words and phrases, will make you think about and remember your purpose statement.

◁ Your purpose statement covers all the aspects of your life as God calls you to be a whole person in His service. ▷

Having a clearly written purpose statement you can keep in front of you is a helpful tool. This purpose statement isn't a job description. It's not tied to your career or current job. It's not a task list, and it does not change from job to job. It's your purpose, not your career. But it is applicable to every career or job or ministry you'll ever have!

I'm not telling you this to overwhelm you. It sounds like a daunting task to come up with something that will guide everything you do for the rest of your life. I'm telling you this to help you think about your big dreams, your goals, and your skills, everything you've discovered throughout this CareerMap. Craft a statement that will keep you focused on your overall life purpose.

Your purpose statement covers all the aspects of your life as God calls you to be a whole person in His service. Let's get started!

First, Go Big-Picture

Answer these questions about your passions, your actions in your community and in the world:

What brings you excitement and energy in or about the

world? (Hint: What do you already spend a lot of time and energy on?)

What really bothers you or angers you in the world? What do you feel needs to change? What would make the world a better place if something stopped or started?

◁ **HINTS** ▷

Think about what you detest the most, and often what you value the most will be the direct opposite of what you hate.

What do you find yourself giving tips or advice about?

If you could coach or train others about what brings you passion and energy, what three or four things would you teach? What is so important to you that you would be willing to roll up your sleeves and get involved? Serve? Build?

How could you use your energy and passion to counteract/minimize what bothers you the most? Make a list of four or five things to determine unique ways you could impact the world.

Service and Volunteer Activities

Now, still think big but get a little more specific. Think about the people represented in your ideas and dreams above. God calls us to serve people, not just ideas.

We can't reach everyone, but we can reach who God has set before us or put in our hearts. So now you're answering that question, "Who has God put in my heart?"

Who would you prefer to serve based on some of your answers from above? The elderly? The young? The poor? Immigrants? The mentally or physically challenged? Healthy or sick people? Addicts? The wealthy? Leaders? Employers? Teachers? The hungry? The list can be as long as you want it to be!

Who would you most enjoy working with or in advocacy for?

Now for the How

In what ways would you help them? Caregiving? Visiting? Writing? Taking care of their animals or property? Building or decorating their homes? Creating custom art for them? Teaching, encouraging, leading? Restoring health? Making their cars safe? Helping others have healthy food to eat? Keeping a building safe? Inventing? Designing health-enhancing tech? Designing safer cars? Building HR systems to support workers? Union leadership? Leading in a church, a youth group, a campus group, a marriage ministry, an elderly group? An international group?

Causes and Advocacy

Is there some existing cause that really matters to you? Perhaps you've already identified this in the what energizes you most and what bothers you most question above. If not, explore more deeply.

Here are some examples of causes many are already working on and maybe you are, too: high school dropouts, animal rights, energy conservation, civil rights, nutrition education, legal advocacy, the homeless, healthcare education, child protection, foster care, adoption, human trafficking, peace, freedom, family education, historic preservation, homeland security, music and the arts, full-time church ministry, missions.

Again, the list is as long as you want it to be. What is something unique that only you could bring to these efforts? This is the what and why of your purpose.

Just Some Brainstorming

By examining for yourself these answers, along with everything else you've discovered in your checkpoints, you can craft your purpose statement. Think about what drives you to do what you do. What helps you wake up in the morning and get out of bed?

Write as many of those words as you can think of and then circle the five that are most important to you or stand out to you. Consider how you might incorporate those words into your purpose statement.

- What passions and actions already mean something to you?
- What service (and for whom) most fits those passions and actions?
- What causes do you feel strongly enough to support and stand for?

You're on your way to knowing your specific mission, the everyday miracles you can bring into this world for the individuals and groups God has fashioned you to serve. Why are we doing all this? Because if you believe that you were created on purpose for a purpose, the sooner you discover that purpose, the more God can use you to serve others.

Now, don't freak out; creating your purpose statement for your specific mission right now doesn't mean that you can't ever change it. You'll probably be tweaking your purpose statement throughout your life, adding to it or clarifying it. You'll learn through unique experiences and opportunities and, as you learn and grow, you'll keep one eye on that purpose statement and adjust as you go.

If you know your purpose and record it, you will have a compass as God speaks to you and works through you. It's an anchor and a way to listen for God's next step and your next little yes to Him as you grow deeper in Him and with your purpose. The enemy will lie, try to steal your joy, and convince you to believe that it is all in your head, rather than in your heart from God.

Sometimes if we are not careful, we can deviate from the purpose and talents God is asking us to use. I confess. It has taken me several years to write this book. I know in my heart it will reach at least one person God is calling to mighty victories. But frankly, I have put it off at times, and I permitted the enemy to get in the way. Sometimes I have acted as my own worst enemy. Don't we all?

I've made excuses, but learn from me: I have missed many blessings from God because I have not obeyed as quickly as I should have. I often think about how much impact I could have on you and others had I completed this work years earlier. When God asks you to co-partner with Him, don't delay as I did. Give Him a yes right away—even if it is a little yes—and then keep going. You must know your purpose and talents and use them for Him to take you to the next step.

Don't forget, no matter what happens, where you go, or what you do: You have a unique purpose to fill.

Jesus, after He rose from the dead and before He ascended back into Heaven, instructed His followers to go out on purpose. He promised that He would be with them each step of the way. He said:

"But you will receive power when the Holy Spirit comes on you; and you will be my witnesses in Jerusalem, and in all Judea and Samaria, and to the ends of the earth" (Acts 1:8).

"But you will receive power when the Holy Spirit comes on you; and you will be my witnesses in Jerusalem, and in all Judea and Samaria, and to the ends of the earth."
—Acts 1:8

What this means is you could be called in your purpose to serve close to home in your own city, you might be called to another place you have never been in, or he might even call you to another country.

My brother was called to Spain as a missionary, my sister called to another state in the medical field, and I was called locally to serve where I grew up. Same inner-city family, serving in different ways.

When you use your naturally given gifts, talents, strengths, small but faithfully determined like David, God supercharges them in wonderful ways that we cannot grasp. If you let Him! When we say yes to the little step by step actions in faith, and when we let God lead, we can watch in amazement at what He accomplishes.

Are you willing to say yes to each small and progressive faithful step that He is asking of you?

David slayed a giant and went on to lead a nation. But it all started with a small yes to be a shepherd, a small yes to trust God, a small yes to build a purpose statement.

◁ Checkpoint #8: Your Purpose Statement ▷

Remember, you don't have to make this purpose statement perfect today. You'll keep working on it and tweaking it throughout the coming seasons of life. But here's where you get to start. It doesn't have to be good. Just use this space to dream and imagine and brainstorm.

Let's think about words. Exciting words. Action words. Verbs. Why? Because you can't fulfill your purpose by just sitting on the couch all day. You gotta get some verbs in there! Below is a list of action verbs that can get you started thinking about what you're going to do to fulfill your purpose. Identify three to five action verbs that best describe you, your skills, talents, or service to help you hone the definition of your unique purpose and goal. You'll want to include these words in your purpose statement.

Action Words—Sample List

Acquire
Administer
Advance
Advocate
Alleviate
Allocate
Author
Beautify
Believe
Bless
Brighten
Broaden
Build
Collaborate
Comfort
Command
Communicate
Compel
Compose
Conceive
Connect
Construct
Convince

Counsel
Create
Defend
Delight
Deliver
Demonstrate
Design
Develop
Educate
Eliminate
Encourage
Engage
Engineer
Enhance
Enlighten
Entertain
Establish
Evaluate
Expand
Facilitate
Follow
Forgive
Foster

Further
Generate
Give
Heal
Help
Host
Illuminate
Imagine
Improvise
Increase
Initiate
Inspire
Integrate
Invent
Involve
Lead
Lighten
Make
Measure
Mediate
Model
Motivate
Negotiate

Network
Nurture
Open
Orchestrate
Organize
Participate
Perfect
Persuade
Practice
Praise
Produce
Promote
Provide
Recognize
Reduce
Reflect
Reform
Relate
Renew
Respect
Restore
Sacrifice
Satisfy

Sell
Serve
Share
Solve
Speak
Stand
Support
Sustain
Teach
Team
Tell
Touch
Train
Transition
Translate
Travel
Understand
Unify
Utilize
Validate
Volunteer
Work
Write

List the five verbs that most excite you:

1. ____________________
2. ____________________
3. ____________________
4. ____________________
5. ____________________

Putting all of this into a two- or three-sentence statement can be an exercise of your heart and soul. Your life purpose statement should encompass all aspects of your life, not just a single career.

To help you see the connection to your career, look at the samples of life purpose statements with connected careers or ministries below.

Sample Purpose Statements

"To discover, uphold, and support trust, honesty, and ethical integrity serving as an advocate with all levels of relationships."—*HR professional, executive leader, or pastor*

"To create, nurture, and maintain a safe environment of learning, growth, and support in challenges for the continuous development of all those around me."—*stay-at-home mom, teacher, or trainer*

"To marvel in every sunrise and sunset, and look for the smallest joys life has to offer in everyday activities in support of those we care for."—*medical or hospice professionals*

"To foster innovation, enhance partnerships and collaborations, and to co-create prosperity and security for all whom I serve."—*entrepreneur, finance executive, or church leader*

And here's my personal purpose statement:
"To build influential, inspiring, character-based leaders, encouraging, supporting those they lead to recognize and live out their own unique life purpose in their workplaces and in ministry."

Take a shot at creating your life purpose statement based on what you've discovered thus far:

Now, get your calendar and mark a day three months from now to revisit this statement. Then, you'll ask yourself: How did it morph into something bigger or different as you learned more about yourself?

God will help you keep learning and tweaking this for the rest of your life as you grow with Him in service to others.

9 Your Personal Board of Directors

YOU'VE BEEN on quite a journey through this CareerMap! You've researched and identified your skills, talents, passions, energizers, and de-energizers, your personality, your style, and what you want more or less of in the world. Now you get to "kick the tires" on your unique purpose and search for work (volunteer or career) that will help you live out your God-given calling.

You've spent most of the time in these pages looking at the big picture, about who you are as a whole person. But here's where you get to go specific. You're going to think about the specific places and people you need to help you fulfill your purpose. First, let's think about some specific aspects of an environment that might fit you well.

In my experience as a leadership and career coach, one of the things I hear the most is that people don't really know what they want in their first or even later careers or ministries. And many tell me what they really don't want to do—which, as you've seen, is a clue to what you like to do because it's the opposite of what you hate to do!

For example, I love talking with and coaching people, so you wouldn't expect me to like sitting in an office alone in front of a computer all day with no one close by. I hate an environment where I am alone and focusing on technology in isolation all day. I do not enjoy environments where people are mean to each other, bickering, or arguing, or nit-picking. I prefer environments where people care and support one another. I love being in and around groups and teams that get along.

From this knowledge I have of myself, I know I should not look for isolating jobs or perhaps hyper-competitive environments. I know I will be drained by those types of environments. I won't last long in those jobs and they do not help me fulfill my personal purpose statement of inspiring leaders and helping people fulfill their unique purpose.

◁ **BRAINSTORM** ▷

Make a working list of careers with your personality type:

Think about this for yourself. Given what you now know about yourself from the checkpoints throughout this book, what kind of environments might work for you? What conditions won't work for you? This is important as you think about career or ministry environments that match you and your unique purpose. Think back to other jobs, volunteer work, or school environments where you were really encouraged and strengthened. What aspects of those environments energized you? What drained you?

Okay, now with all the checkpoints you have completed thus far, flip to the "Resources" at back of this book to find "Careers with Your Personality Type," that list of personalities and careers from chapter two. What jobs or career paths might fit in with your purpose statement, your personality, your values and skills, your passions, and even your environmental preferences? Choose a few from that list, and add whatever comes to your mind. Do some brainstorming here.

Time For a Test Drive

You can begin to better serve and learn where you best fit for your purpose. By becoming a bit of a scientist, you can experiment. Or if you like cars like I do, it's time to go out for a test drive to validate your purpose.

You may try some volunteer work or ministry first to see how the role fits. Does it bring you energy? Or does it drain you? If it drains you, it may mean that you have to try a different aspect that still fits your purpose, in a different setting or with different leadership style. That said, try anything for a period of time and give it some time. It takes time to learn and get comfortable so you will probably be somewhat uncomfortable in the beginning

This "best fit" check will be very important as you gain skills and confidence in where God is leading you. God will grow your purpose and your influence network to higher levels of your purpose as you continue to listen, grow, and learn.

Terrified in Action

For example, when I was trying to figure out where I could best fit with my love of coaching and training wonderful people like you on how to find their first career, I consented to becoming the student president of my counseling graduate program.

Since I was told by many that I was good at gathering people, I selected my own team of counseling students to help me to run the student organization.

Our student team noticed there wasn't a lot of support in finding a place to complete their internship required for earning the master's degree. So we decided to split up and look for employers to participate in our first internship career fair. We began with somewhat outdated information, which led to us other connections out in the counseling world. We eventually convinced eighteen employers to come and join us in a career fair event for our students. We had food and fun as the students visited the separate employer tables and provided their résumés and transcripts to potential internship sites. Our mentors and senior faculty were also in attendance to support and to see what we had accomplished.

In this activity, I learned how to create and run a program with a team. I learned how to approach strangers and invite them to something that they would gain from, as well as help the students to learn on the job and fulfill the requirements to graduate. People helping people on both sides of the equation is something I love. Even though I was scared to death, I did it anyway! I later learned how to increase my skills in developing programs, how to manage teams, and to help people learn and grow.

Through this experience and others like it, I learned that I was pretty good at program management and coaching others on how to be successful in teams.

Way later, I was put in charge of multiple leadership development programs from new leaders up to executive level coaching. I found I loved doing this. I used my people skills, my organization skills, and my love of strategically helping people to be even more successful within their purpose and lives!

If you were to have told me that I would be able to lead leaders like this in the beginning of my purpose journey, I would have told you "No way! I am not good enough or skilled enough." And yet, with each little yes when God asked me to try something new at another level, He walked with me in my fear and grew my talents to serve Him and others in ways that energized me.

He brought me to higher levels of influence for the next little yes that God asked of me.

Writing this book is one of the little yeses that God asked me to complete—to assist you the way He guided me. You can do this! With God's help you can change lives in ways you can't even imagine right now. No matter what age or stage of life you are in, say yes to the first step God is asking of you. The step of completing this CareerMap, seeking your own unique purpose no matter what stage of life you are in, could be a new beginning—a little yes God has asked of you. There's still one last question: How?

The answer lies in those letters, H, O, and W, but we're going to rearrange them: W-H-O! Who do you know that can help you make connections and find where you fit?

Your Personal Board of Directors—Wise Counsel to Assist You

First, think about your immediate friends. Who might help by making connections for you? Even if you don't think anyone in your immediate circle of friends could directly help you, your friends have friends. And their friends have friends, and so on. Other people can help you make connections to assist you in what will fulfill your unique purpose. To use an old adage—it's a small world!

"Plans fail for lack of counsel, but with many advisers they succeed."
—*Proverbs 15:22*

But you aren't just out to build relationships for what they can do for you. No, your connections are valuable way beyond the jobs or careers you might find through them. (This is a concept called net-giving—we'll talk about that in the next chapter!)

Many, if not most, organizations have boards of people to help them make decisions effectively. Each board member or leader contributes counsel to decisions and commitments made for the company. Usually the board members represent a range of knowledge, careers, skills, background experience, and personalities.

Your Personal Board of Directors is where you keep a group of people who are cheering for you, assisting you, and encouraging you. You will need advisors to help you see things you can't see. They will hold you accountable, give you counsel and feedback, and support you as you explore opportunities in light of your calling and purpose. Your friends will help you find your best fit through both choosing what you love and help you stay away from things that drain you and don't fit you.

Your PBD needs to be comprised of people you trust, preferably who share your faith and have your best interest at heart. Some of these are life-long role models from your past who can still guide you. Others will show up when needed at each stage of your calling and purpose.

Intentionality is key to building your PBD. You get to choose who you trust and who has your best interest at heart. To get you thinking, here are some people I chose and what they bring to my life and how they ended up on my intentionally crafted Personal Board of Directors.

Bob P.—God used Bob, my college department chair who saw leadership skills within me when I didn't. He helped me believe in my calling for leadership, growing me through various stages of leadership in my life. Not just at work, by the way, but in all of life! I claimed him as an adopted dad. He was my first professional leadership mentor, sponsor, trainer, and coach for twenty years.

Grandma C. is a role model I'm still learning from. She's my adopted mom, not that she legally adopted me, but that I claimed her as my mom when I needed a faith-driven role model. She was a spitfire champion of the weak and built me to be strong. I didn't see her very often, but she was always (and still is) in my heart. And she taught me quilting, so in every aspect of my life I make connection patterns with people and fabric.

Alicia B. is a former employee, but now she is a co-laborer, partner, one of my editors, and my dearest friend and listener. She taught me everything I know about visual communication and training materials. She is the introvert to my overzealous extrovert. She has been the best sounding board for me on ideas and plans. Interestingly, our lives have intersected by coincidence (God winks) in three different settings of my life, unbeknownst to either of us!

Emily G. is my millennial friend and editor for this book! I "accidentally" met her at a coffee shop—God is so cool! (God wink!) So is Emily. She is a great storytelling coach who assists people in sharing their unique story. She also is an advocate, voice, and thinking partner for the millennial and Gen Z perspectives of any work I do. Her input and editing is crucial for me.

Brenda M. is the best social media marketer and net-giver I know. I "accidentally" met her in a career ministry consortium as she trained others on how to market themselves for their next career via social media. She has a large heart for women leaders everywhere!

Nancy S. is my financial advisor. She's a huge support in helping me build my own network and helps me think about net-giving in creative ways. She has also been a rock in my faith to help me stay strong.

Gail S. is one of the most widely known net-givers I have ever met. She never ceases to help others find opportunities and knows everyone on our side of the world. She is a warm, caring human being, constantly and selflessly coaching, giving support, and sharing resources!

I have a total of seven people on my Personal Board of Directors. As you can see, I've often found my PBD members in interesting ways—like seemingly random or chance meetings at coffee shops and through trusted existing contacts.

Now It's Your Turn

In the next Checkpoint exercise, jot down some names that you might consider asking to be on your Personal Board of Directors. These people are friends who have something to give you that you might not have. They might add to your vision because they are big-picture thinkers. Or they may keep your feet on the ground and help you think about nitty-gritty things because they are detail-oriented. They might just be that voice in your corner cheering you on in the middle of the journey. You definitely need at least one of those, if not more!

Take a look at what you're already doing. Volunteer work? Boards, committees, community groups? Professional associations? Hobbies? Support groups, faith-based organizations, alumni associations? Look at the things you're already doing, and see who's there.

Next, think about role models you have had. What drew you to them? Why did you need them in your life and how were they important to you? Who's the most inspirational and influential person you've ever known?

Finally, think about who you want to be—your values, your skills, purpose, and goals—and who is already there, or who might help you get there. Also think about the level of your relationships. Are you giving into these relationships, too?

◃ Checkpoint #9: Your Personal Board of Directors ▹

Use this chart to help you think about who you might ask to be on your PBD. Think about how you can also help each other by net-giving.

Building Your Personal Board of Directors

	Name	Level of Relationship	Specific Skills & Strengths	How You Support Them
Listener, encourager, sounding board				
Reverse mentor (younger than you)				
Role model for shared values				
Supports, coaches your unique purpose				
Network builder (net-giving)				
Financial security mentor				
Executive, leadership sponsor				
Thinking partner				
Prayer, encourager				

This Personal Board of Directors you have created can serve as wise counsel to confirm what God has asked of you within His purpose. Remember, prayer and Scripture is our first line of checking God's will on decisions. Wise counsel (after you talk and listen to what God says) can help guide you in decision making within your purpose.

Going outside of your purpose can lead you astray and cause pain that we all wish to avoid. God is your co-partner in anything He calls you to. Pulling all the clues together—we have just created a map of who you are and what matters to you. Now we need to seek wisdom to make sense of all the unique clues about you.

Who do you know with integrity, strong character, and wisdom who can guide and counsel you as you try on your purpose and calling for size? Who is already on or needs to be added to your Personal Board of Directors?

1. ______________________________
2. ______________________________
3. ______________________________

Choose your PBD members carefully. Learn from them, but because they are human, always check in with God for what He wishes you to do. Make sure you sift advice through God's Word before you act. So finally, with all your clues so far…

Where might you like to serve?

What kinds of people will assist you?

How will you serve?

How will you identify where you will serve?

This is where wise counsel can help you, and Scripture can guide you to decisions on your next little yes to God's purpose for you.

10 Net-Giving: Better than Networking

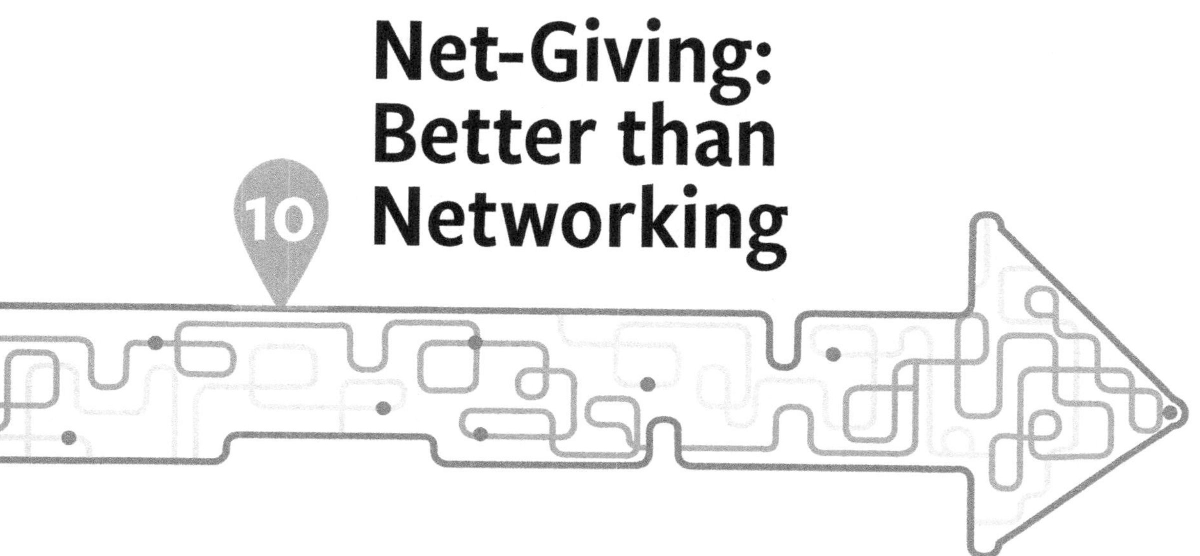

YOU'RE ALL PACKED and ready to go! Well, almost. There's one more thing you need in your suitcase. We've talked about it already, but here's where you get to dream a little about how you could put it into practice.

Net-Giving

It might also be thought of as paying it forward, but it's a little more broad than that. Net-giving is when you assist and serve in others' successes, and in doing so, you add to your own successes. Net-giving creates thinking partners, collaborators, and friends who can (and want to!) help connect you to others and resources.

As I mentioned earlier, another of my favorite authors, Tommy Spaulding, introduced me to the concept of net-giving in *It's Not Just Who You Know*. He has some wonderful personal stories on how his purpose came about in many ways through net-giving, much like in my own life. You may wish to read his book to learn about this topic and how to create high-level relationships that will permit you to succeed in ways that you could never could without the assistance of others.

Net-giving is similar to networking, but it's better. When you network, you meet new people and introduce yourself—and if you're an introvert, it's one of your least favorite things to do. It takes some social grace, some small talk skills, and a fair amount of confidence. Net-giving is similar in that you still do a decent amount of meeting new people, but instead of going into it seeing what you can get out of other people, you go into it seeing how you can *give* to others.

"Give, and it will be given to you. A good measure, pressed down, shaken together and running over, will be poured into your lap. For with the measure you use, it will be measured to you."

—Luke 6:38

And in my mind, net-giving is the best way to do a test drive on what fits you. Experiment with what charges your batteries and what makes your heart sing while genuinely serving others at the same time. But here's the catch: net-giving doesn't operate on a give-to-get basis. It's not a you-scratch-my-back-and-I'll-scratch-yours thing. It's a bigger concept.

Jesus says, "It is more blessed to give than to receive" (Acts 20:35).

Through giving, God promises to give back to us. As Luke 6:38 says, "Give, and it will be given to you. A good measure, pressed down, shaken together and running over, will be poured into your lap. For with the measure you use it will be measured to you."

You might not get to choose how or when or what you receive, but He will give back to you through others. Keep in mind that we may not receive from the ones we have served but rather from someone else. That's what God has created us for; serving one another, giving to someone in need, and receiving what we need from someone else. It's an intricate connection of support through the giving of our God-given skills, talents, and strengths to support what we were designed for: to serve one another.

Jesus modeled this with His disciples in the past, and He still does this with us today. He served alongside the disciples and gave His very life for us—even though He didn't deserve to die.

In addition to service, when we invest in others and care about their successes, we both learn and teach each other. Just as the disciples learned and grew in their faith together. We all gain from our acts of service while increasing the connections of relationship. Our own success is dependent not just on our own efforts, but through others' service and support—and vice versa.

Net-giving works on your behalf and steers you toward strategies that help make new experiences happen. In the last chapter, I talked about how I assisted in helping my fellow counseling students to help themselves by creating an opportunity for them to find their own internships through service and connections.

Others benefited from what I provided for them, while I learned more of what God wanted from me in my purpose to serve others. That's the beauty of net-giving. The students gained an opportunity to graduate and also to find their first mentor (perhaps the beginning of their Personal Board of Directors). The residual gain for me was learning more about what I was capable of in real time action—not sitting on the sidelines, staying scared to try something I had never experienced before. I grew and learned more about myself and what I was capable of through serving someone else with God's guidance.

It was my first little yes to God, even when I was afraid and didn't believe I could lead others.

What were your answers to "What really bothers you or angers you in the world? What do you feel needs to change? What would make the world a better place if something stopped or started something new?"

Who are you going to serve? Where would you like to serve? Using what talents?

God has created you uniquely. He has called all of us to

serve one another as Jesus served His disciples and followers, both then and now, through the Holy Spirit's leading.

God will work in your life as you obey His prompting and nudges to guide you. God is patient as we find our way and allows for stretches of learning time between each little yes. You must be patient with yourself as you grapple and sometimes stumble while trying to find your unique purpose. Remember God's purpose is two-fold for your life: One part is to grow you in your own walk with Him in your faith. The other part—even more important—is for you to serve others and assist them in their learning and service. By doing so, we help others learn and live their purpose. It's service—simply what God has called us to do. The choice to say yes is always up to you.

If you have accepted Christ, and therefore God's calling and purpose for your life which morphs and grows with each little yes, you will be blessed beyond what you can imagine.

Obedient service leads to patient faith. Faith leads to God's blessings, blessings lead to learning, and others benefit from our service.

A gentle warning from own life: I delayed listening to God's ask for my first little yes for many years. I tried to do things my own way. I didn't truly submit my life until I was in my late 30s. He eventually led me to my purpose, but there are times when I regret I didn't listen to God much earlier. I am sure I have missed many opportunities that I might have had because of my delay in obedience.

Remember what we learned from Matthew 25—it's risky to not use our talents.

◁ Checkpoint #10: Your Net-Giving ▷

Here's where you get to do some dreaming! Imagine you have your dream job, and you're in charge of all your time and have been given permission to go help people. You get to choose who and how. But here's the catch: you're not allowed to spend money. Net-giving doesn't require money! It only requires a genuine spirit that is willing to spend time to build someone else's success. It requires humility and selflessness, but it doesn't require wealth.

So here's your final checkpoint: Plan and dream some ideas on how you will net-give! Who will you be looking for? What kinds of people are you most passionate about helping? Dream and brainstorm some ways you can net-give now and in the future.

How is net-giving different than networking?

What are you doing right now to give back or serve others? Think about your time volunteering, serving on committees, student memberships, professional associations, or in common-interest clubs.

What skills have you already discovered that could aid you in net-giving?

1. ______
2. ______
3. ______
4. ______
5. ______

Without spending money, what are ways that you can serve and net-give?

1. ______
2. ______
3. ______

Who do you want to serve?

1. ______
2. ______
3. ______

How does net-giving help you see new ways to serve people and God? How does it create opportunities for new experiences in careers or ministry?

A Final Send-off

Together we have completed many checkpoints to explore your purpose—your talents, strengths, natural knacks, activities that energize, fuel your passions and purpose—all the good stuff God created you with.

Realistically, though, we have one more aspect of life that greatly influences our purpose. We have all experienced challenges, disappointments, and suffering within our lives. Yet from these experiences, although not pleasant, sometimes comes the most clarity and the building of character within us, which can lead to a deep purpose.

Romans 5:3–5 tells us, "But we also glory in our sufferings, because we know that suffering produces perseverance; perseverance, character; and character, hope. And hope does not put us to shame, because God's love has been poured out into our hearts through the Holy Spirit, who has been given to us."

In challenging times, we can use what we have learned through our trials as well as our skills to meet the needs of others.

Use your clues and your past or present challenges to assist you to find your own unique purpose!

Warmly,

Cathy McCafferty-Smith

Resources

◁ Careers with Your Personality Type ▷

You can find a career or ministry that uses your talents and personality—a perfect fit that will energize you and not drain you.

After you complete Chapter Two and learn about your personality type, take a look at the sixteen lists on the following pages. One of these will match your four-letter personality type. You'll find a list of the careers that typically work well with your personality type. It's okay to dream a little bit. Look around at all of the careers and personality types. It's okay if you see careers that interest you in the other types.

If you find careers that pique your interest, talk to someone who is already in that career. Ask them about their job and their personality type. Perhaps you could find volunteer or internship opportunities in these careers. Keep exploring to find what God has purposefully and plan-fully prepared for you! This exploration will continue your whole life as you develop your skills and clarify what is important.

Charts on the following pages:

ISTJ

Possible Career/Ministry Choices

ISTJs can find career satisfaction in different areas than what is listed here. The key is what fits your talents, skills, values, and what you enjoy doing most. This includes anything that builds on the uniqueness of your ISTJ letter preferences.

Possible Fields of Interest

- o Aviation
- o Economics
- o Construction
- o Dentistry
- o Educational administration
- o Engineering: industrial, petroleum, nuclear
- o Engineering: civil, mechanical
- o Law Enforcement and other protective services
- o Manufacturing
- o Management: office and executive
- o Management and Supervision: building, construction, agriculture
- o Military
- o Nursing and healthcare administration
- o Purchasing
- o Teaching: trades, technical, math

Add any additional fields of interest below you may have seen from the other lists that interest or energize you.

ISFJ

Possible Career/Ministry Choices

ISFJs can find career satisfaction in different areas than what is listed here. The key is what fits your talents, skills, values, and what you enjoy doing most. This includes anything that builds on the uniqueness of your ISFJ letter preferences.

Possible Fields of Interest

- o Bookkeeping and bank teller
- o Dental hygiene
- o Dietician and nutrition specialist
- o Corrections and probation
- o Hotel/motel lodging manager and clerk
- o Health education and services
- o Library and information service professions
- o Medical technology
- o Medicine: family and general practice
- o Nursing: registered, licenses practical
- o Office support, data entry, word processing
- o Paralegal
- o Physical therapy
- o Religious professions
- o Secretary and administrative assistant
- o Social service administration
- o Teaching pre-k through elementary

Add any additional fields of interest below you may have seen from the other lists that interest or energize you.

INTJ

Possible Career/Ministry Choices

INTJs can find career satisfaction in different areas than what is listed here. The key is what fits your talents, skills, values, and what you enjoy doing most. This includes anything that builds on the uniqueness of your INTJ letter preferences.

Possible Fields of Interest

- o Arts and entertainment: actor, musician, composer
- o Computer sciences
- o Economics
- o Engineering: nuclear, electrical, aeronautical, computer, materials
- o Executive and manager: sciences
- o Executive and manager: military, protective services
- o Human resources
- o Law: lawyer, judge
- o Management consulting
- o Medicine: internal, pathology, research
- o Multimedia arts and design
- o Photography
- o Physical, life, and social sciences
- o Research
- o College professor
- o Writing, editing, journalism

Add any additional fields of interest below you may have seen from the other lists that interest or energize you.

INFJ

Possible Career/Ministry Choices

INFJs can find career satisfaction in different areas than what is listed here. The key is what fits your talents, skills, values, and what you enjoy doing most. This includes anything that builds on the uniqueness of your INFJ letter preferences.

Possible Fields of Interest

- o Architecture
- o Counseling and psychotherapy
- o Educational consulting
- o Engineering: biomedical, petroleum
- o Environmental sciences
- o Fine arts, graphic design, multimedia
- o Dental hygiene
- o Interior design
- o Librarian, information sciences
- o Marketing
- o Medicine: family practice, psychiatry, pathology, surgery
- o Occupational therapy
- o Religious professions
- o Research, writing
- o Performing arts
- o Physician Assistant
- o Psychology
- o Teaching
- o Vocational education

Add any additional fields of interest below you may have seen from the other lists that interest or energize you.

ISTP

Possible Career/Ministry Choices

ISTPs can find career satisfaction in different areas than what is listed here. The key is what fits your talents, skills, values, and what you enjoy doing most. This includes anything that builds on the uniqueness of your ISTP letter preferences.

Possible Fields of Interest

- o Forestry
- o Agriculture
- o Farming and Ranching
- o Construction and trades: carpentry, electrical, other
- o Military, law enforcement, corrections
- o Aviation: air crew, assembler, mechanic
- o Engineering: electrical, mechanical, computer hardware and software
- o Electrical, electronics, telecommunications installation and repair
- o Geology and geophysics
- o Computer sciences
- o Machinist, plant operations
- o Law: lawyer, legal administration
- o Physical therapy
- o Accounting
- o Manager, administrator, small business, government, social services
- o Teaching: adult education, coaching

Add any additional fields of interest below you may have seen from the other lists that interest or energize you.

ISFP

Possible Career/Ministry Choices

ISFPs can find career satisfaction in different areas than what is listed here. The key is what fits your talents, skills, values, and what you enjoy doing most. This includes anything that builds on the uniqueness of your ISFP letter preferences.

Possible Fields of Interest

- o Veterinary medicine
- o Nursing, medical technology
- o Applied engineering specialties and engineering technician
- o Surveying and gardening
- o Office and administrative support
- o Personal care and services
- o Computer operations and data analysis
- o Physical therapy
- o Bookkeeping
- o Medicine: obstetrics, gynecology, pediatrics, family medicine
- o Transportation, aviation
- o Recreation and coaching
- o Religious education
- o Teaching: K-12
- o Storekeeper
- o Law enforcement: detective
- o Crafts and trades: carpenter, electrician, other trades

Add any additional fields of interest below you may have seen from the other lists that interest or energize you.

INFP

Possible Career/Ministry Choices

INFPs can find career satisfaction in different areas than what is listed here. The key is what fits your talents, skills, values, and what you enjoy doing most. This includes anything that builds on the uniqueness of your INFP letter preferences.

Possible Fields of Interest

- o Fine artist
- o Interior design
- o Visual arts, graphic design, multimedia, animation
- o Psychologist: clinical, counseling, educational
- o Counseling, social work, community services
- o Medicine: psychiatry
- o Architecture
- o Writing and editing
- o Journalism and publishing
- o Religious professions
- o Social sciences, research
- o Educational consulting
- o Personal care and services
- o Physical therapy
- o Teaching: arts, drama, music, English
- o Performing arts and entertainment
- o Musician, singer, composer
- o Social and life sciences, public health

Add any additional fields of interest below you may have seen from the other lists that interest or energize you.

INTP

Possible Career/Ministry Choices

INTPs can find career satisfaction in different areas than what is listed here. The key is what fits your talents, skills, values, and what you enjoy doing most. This includes anything that builds on the uniqueness of your INTP letter preferences.

Possible Fields of Interest

- o Computing and systems administration
- o Architecture
- o Fine arts
- o Graphic design, photography
- o Life and physical sciences: biology, chemistry, geology
- o Social sciences
- o Political sciences
- o Information sciences, research
- o Law, attorney, judge
- o Journalism, writing, and editing
- o Executive: law, computing, construction
- o Psychology: industrial, organizational
- o Acting, entertainment, directing
- o Pharmacy
- o Engineering: biomedical, software, aerospace, civil, other
- o Medicine: pathology, psychiatry, other
- o Electronics

Add any additional fields of interest below you may have seen from the other lists that interest or energize you.

ESTP

Possible Career/Ministry Choices

ESTPs can find career satisfaction in different areas than what is listed here. The key is what fits your talents, skills, values, and what you enjoy doing most. This includes anything that builds on the uniqueness of your ESTP letter preferences.

Possible Fields of Interest

- o Marketing and sales
- o Law enforcement: police officer and detective
- o Construction and carpentry
- o Protective services: firefighter, other
- o Aviation and transportation: pilot, air crew, driver
- o Military careers
- o Forestry: gardening, farming, fishing
- o Credit investigator and loan officer
- o Banking, business, and finance
- o Tax examiner and auditor
- o Reporter and editor
- o Machinist and mechanic
- o Electrical or electronic repair
- o Pharmacy
- o Real estate and insurance sales
- o Business management
- o Bartending, chef, and cook
- o Management and supervision: military, agriculture, trades

Add any additional fields of interest below you may have seen from the other lists that interest or energize you.

ESFP

Possible Career/Ministry Choices

ESFPs can find career satisfaction in different areas than what is listed here. The key is what fits your talents, skills, values, and what you enjoy doing most. This includes anything that builds on the uniqueness of your ESFP letter preferences.

Possible Fields of Interest

- o Healthcare and healthcare support
- o Medical technology
- o Respiratory therapy
- o Hospitality and lodging
- o Fitness and training
- o Sales
- o Social services, counseling
- o Veterinary medicine
- o Child care
- o Recreation, coaching, and lifeguard
- o Religious education
- o Nursing
- o Construction and trades
- o Transportation
- o Pharmacology
- o Cosmetology
- o Library worker
- o Outdoor careers: gardening, forestry, farming, fishing
- o Office administration, support, bookkeeping

Add any additional fields of interest below you may have seen from the other lists that interest or energize you.

ENFP

Possible Career/Ministry Choices

ENFPs can find career satisfaction in different areas than what is listed here. The key is what fits your talents, skills, values, and what you enjoy doing most. This includes anything that builds on the uniqueness of your ENFP letter preferences.

Possible Fields of Interest

- o Entertainment: acting, directing
- o Fine arts and visual arts
- o Music and composing
- o Psychology: clinical, counseling, educational
- o Counseling and social work
- o Hospitality and lodging
- o Journalism and writing
- o Religious professions education
- o Social sciences
- o Healthcare and healthcare support
- o Teaching: arts, adult education
- o Cosmetology
- o Sales
- o Public relations
- o Computing
- o Photography
- o Education: administration, consulting
- o Forestry
- o Landscape architecture
- o Child care

Add any additional fields of interest below you may have seen from the other lists that interest or energize you.

ENTP

Possible Career/Ministry Choices

ENTPs can find career satisfaction in different areas than what is listed here. The key is what fits your talents, skills, values, and what you enjoy doing most. This includes anything that builds on the uniqueness of your ENTP letter preferences.

Possible Fields of Interest

- o Arts and entertainment, theater
- o Manager and executive: arts, entertainment
- o Journalism, visual arts, photography
- o Life and physical sciences, geology, biology, chemistry, economy
- o Social sciences
- o Marketing and public relations
- o Finance
- o Executive: business, finance, healthcare
- o Human resources
- o Computing: analyst, programmer,
- o Management consulting
- o Sales and advertising
- o Psychology: industrial/organizational
- o Engineering: industrial/organizational, electrical, chemical
- o Architecture
- o Executive: architecture, engineering, transportation, production
- o Computer and electrical technician
- o Construction and skilled trades

Add any additional fields of interest below you may have seen from the other lists that interest or energize you.

ESTJ

Possible Career/Ministry Choices

ESTJs can find career satisfaction in different areas than what is listed here. The key is what fits your talents, skills, values, and what you enjoy doing most. This includes anything that builds on the uniqueness of your ESTJ letter preferences.

Possible Fields of Interest

- o Protective services: law enforcement, firefighting, corrections
- o Management: general
- o Management and supervision: mechanics, agriculture, construction
- o Production and manufacturing: technician, operations, supervision
- o Accounting
- o Banking and finance
- o Purchasing
- o Administration: education, healthcare
- o Construction and trades
- o Teaching: trades and technical
- o Executive and manager: transportation, building, grounds
- o Management consulting
- o Military
- o Engineering: civil, mechanical, chemical
- o Aviation: pilot
- o Law: judge

Add any additional fields of interest below you may have seen from the other lists that interest or energize you.

ESFJ

Possible Career/Ministry Choices

ESFJs can find career satisfaction in different areas than what is listed here. The key is what fits your talents, skills, values, and what you enjoy doing most. This includes anything that builds on the uniqueness of your ESFJ letter preferences.

Possible Fields of Interest

- o Medical technology
- o Lodging and hospitality
- o Healthcare: dental, pediatrics, family practice, surgical
- o Management and supervision: healthcare, child care
- o Nursing
- o Religious professions
- o Religious education
- o Childcare
- o Office and administration support
- o Personal trainer
- o Cosmetology
- o Community and social services
- o Teaching: preschool, kindergarten, elementary
- o Teaching: vocational education
- o Speech pathology
- o Public health and health education
- o Educational: student personnel
- o Landscaping and gardening

Add any additional fields of interest below you may have seen from the other lists that interest or energize you.

ENFJ

Possible Career/Ministry Choices

ENFJs can find career satisfaction in different areas than what is listed here. The key is what fits your talents, skills, values, and what you enjoy doing most. This includes anything that builds on the uniqueness of your ENFJ letter preferences.

Possible Fields of Interest

- o Religious professions and education
- o Psychology, mental health counseling
- o Community services and social work
- o Fine arts and craft artist
- o Arts and entertainment: actor, musician, composer
- o Interior design
- o Photography
- o Teaching: art, drama, music, English, languages
- o Lodging and hospitality and events and convention planning
- o Medicine: family, general practice, psychiatry, other
- o Writing and journalism
- o Marketing, public relations, sales
- o Home healthcare, child care
- o Social and political sciences
- o Dental hygiene
- o Management and administration: education, personal services

Add any additional fields of interest below you may have seen from the other lists that interest or energize you.

ENTJ

Possible Career/Ministry Choices

ENTJs can find career satisfaction in different areas than what is listed here. The key is what fits your talents, skills, values, and what you enjoy doing most. This includes anything that builds on the uniqueness of your ENTJ letter preferences.

Possible Fields of Interest

- o Engineering: electrical, chemical, other
- o Law: attorney, judge
- o Life, physical, social sciences: biology, geology, chemistry, psychology
- o Executive and manager: sciences, computer
- o Business and finance
- o Executive and manager: business, finance, operations
- o Marketing, sales
- o Human resources
- o Computing: analyst, systems administration
- o Executive and manager: education, health, community services
- o Urban planning
- o Skill trades
- o Production and manufacturing
- o Management and consulting
- o College professor
- o Psychology: industrial, organizational

Add any additional fields of interest below you may have seen from the other lists that interest or energize you.

◁ Additional Resources ▷

I have found these resources to be helpful in my own adventure of seeking a calling and purpose, and in guiding others to find theirs. These authors have inspired and taught me many things in my own purpose journey. I recommend these resources as you seek your purpose in work and ministry.

Anyway—The Paradoxical Commandments: Finding Personal Meaning in a Crazy World by Kent M. Keith. Learn to focus on what God has taught us, "love them—anyway," and "give the world the best you have—anyway."

Becoming a Person of Influence: How to Positively Impact the Lives of Others by John Maxwell, who also authored *Wisdom from Women in Bible: Giants of the Faith Speak Into Our Lives.*

The Butterfly Effect: How Your Life Matters by Andy Andrews. Everything you do matters and impacts. Also see the *The Little Things: Why You Should Really Sweat the Small Stuff*, *The Traveler's Gift*: *Seven Decisions that Determine Personal Success*, and *Seven Decisions: Understanding the Keys to Personal Success*, all by the same author.

The Go Giver: A Little Story About a Powerful Business Idea by Bob Burg and John David Mann. Humble servant leadership in the mission field of business.

Intentional Leadership: 12 Lenses for Focusing Strengths, Managing Weaknesses, and Achieving Your Purpose by Jane Kise. Personality type and intentional leadership.

It's Not Just Who You Know: Transform Your Life (and Your Organization) by Turning Colleagues and Contacts into Lasting, Genuine Relationships by Tommy Spaulding. Building deeper levels of relationship by serving and supporting others.

Living Your Strengths: Discover Your God-Given Talents and Inspire Your Community by Albert Winesman. Identify your strengths and the strengths of others; align your strengths to a ministry or career.

The Godwink Series by SQuire Rushnell and Lousie DuArt. Coincidences, divine alignments, mini-miracles and checkpoints from God.

You Were Born For This: 7 Keys to a Life of Predictable Miracles by Bruce Wilkinson (also the author of *The Prayer of Jabez* and many other books).

◁ Key Scripture References ▷

Throughout this book I have quoted from the Bible (using the New International Version). This is *the book* with proof that God does have a unique plan and purpose for you!

**"Not only so, but we also glory in our sufferings,
because we know that suffering produces perseverance;
perseverance, character; and character, hope.
And hope does not put us to shame, because God's love has been
poured out into our hearts through the Holy Spirit,
who has been given to us."**

—Romans 5:3–5

"For we are God's handiwork, created in Christ Jesus to do good works, which God prepared in advance for us to do."*—Ephesians 2:10*

"'For I know the plans I have for you,' declares the LORD, 'plans to prosper you and not to harm you, plans to give you a hope and a future.'"*—Jeremiah 29:11*

"You will seek me and find me when you seek me with all your heart."
—Jeremiah 29:13

"Plans fail for lack of counsel, but with many advisers they succeed."
—Proverbs 15:22

◁ Acknowledgements ▷

Gratefully, I wish to honor those who helped me shape my own purpose and calling.

Dr. Robert Payne, adopted dad, mentor, and department chair of Human Resources Development at Oakland University. He saw leadership in me when I didn't recognize it myself. He transformed my thinking about what I was capable of doing as a leader.

Alicia Beck, adopted sister and best friend, project coordinator at Oakland Schools. She started as a colleague and became a friend, and now serves as the listening and discernment partner for every idea, career development course, and leadership training session I have developed.

Dr. Howard Splete, adopted uncle, mentor, and Oakland University professor. As co-author of the Global Career Development Facilitator Certification program from the National Career Development Association, he encouraged me to take risks and allowed me to teach university students while earning my master's degree.

Emily Gehman, adopted little sister and storytelling coach. I "accidentally" met Emily in an interesting and miraculous way. As storytelling director at Shattered Media, Inc., she is an awesome millennial mentor who assisted in making this book a better voice to reach more people.

Tonia Harrison, author of *Designed with Your Purpose in Mind: Living the Life God Planned for You.* I met Tonia through some coincidental experiences that led to writing articles for a faith-based blog. These articles became the outlines for some of the chapters in this book. Tonia went home to be with God in 2018. This work is a tribute also to her, and her shared dedication to help others to find their purpose.

Career Transition Ministry Consortium. Many thanks to my fellow partners in the Career Transition Ministry Consortium during the mid-2000s Great Recession, when many lost their jobs but also found their calling and purpose. Dr. Ken Woodside, Marty Miller, Mike Whelan (who also went home to be with God), Jeff Davidson, Alicia Beck, and many others who supported those who were hurting and frightened for their future and assisted in finding careers and ministries within God's next plan for their lives.

Between Successes—Strategic Human Resource Management. My sincere thanks to **Gail Sanderson** and **Rich Spriggle**, who supported the unemployed human resource leaders who had the difficult task of right-sizing their organization, and then often found themselves out of work as well. It was difficult time for many, and yet a time of rediscovery as we learned where God wanted each of us to be in His plan to serve others.

OU Cultivate and International Oasis leadership partners and students are investing in leadership with OU students, helping train young leaders in their faith and service for God and preparing them for ministry or the mission field of today's workplace. Thank you to our leaders and coaches, Rev. Cam Underdown, Rev. D. C. Svenson, Rev. Dale Partin, Janine Iyer, Alexa Lawyor, Alaina Burr, Kiana Keller, Kelly Ray, Kyle Vens, Brian Perry, and many others who are building the next generation of called, purpose-focused servants of God. I have been blessed by each of you through your teaching, as well as through watching you live your own calling!

My kids and grandkids: Carrie, Keith, Alyvia, Brooke, Drew, and **David; Lesley, Evelyn, Emma, and Cole;** and my **husband, Charles**: Thank you to the most important people I love, for allowing me to be me, and for loving me anyway! I am grateful for all of God's blessings—but especially grateful for you, dear ones!

To the reader of this book: May this book, in some small way, assist you in finding and growing within your unique purpose!

◁ My Letter to God ▷

Dear God,

You asked me to write this book, and I told You that I wasn't even sure anyone would even read it. You spoke to my heart and said to write it anyway. So I tried slowly, with many starts and stops over years.

Then one day, I was with my friend Judy, also a writer and storyteller, and we were talking about my greatest hero in the faith, Billy Graham, who had recently passed away at age 99.

I told Judy I was writing a guide to help them see the skills already recognizable in their life, which could help them to discover their unique calling and purpose.

And yet, as I lamented to Judy, I didn't think anyone would read it. Judy asked me if I knew who the individual was who led Billy Graham to the Lord. I didn't know the answer. That one person led Billy Graham to You, God, and who through Your partnership with Billy, that one person changed millions of lives all over the world. Including mine.

One person's little yes to obey You in that pivotal moment made that much difference with Your power, plan, and through their unique purpose!

In that moment, I promised You that I would finish this book—even if only one person's life would be changed as they begin to discover what unique plan You have waiting for them, no matter how old or young they are.

God, I pray that You will put this simple, practical book into that one person's hand in a unique and awe-inspiring way so they know You are with them.

My hope is they will also read Your book, the Bible.

Transform their life, show them their unique calling to serve, help them impact and change others' lives within the unique purpose You have designed just for them.

Thank you, God for helping me write this book.

Amen!

P.S. My dear reader holding this book in your hands—are you the one person for whom God asked me to write?

Made in the USA
Las Vegas, NV
21 May 2023